Anonymous

Rare and Valuable Books, on the History and Literature of the Australian Colonies

Anonymous

Rare and Valuable Books, on the History and Literature of the Australian Colonies

ISBN/EAN: 9783337315306

Printed in Europe, USA, Canada, Australia, Japan

Cover: Foto ©ninafisch / pixelio.de

More available books at **www.hansebooks.com**

CATALOGUE

OF THE COLLECTION OF

Rare and Valuable Books,

ON THE

HISTORY AND LITERATURE

OF THE

AUSTRALIAN COLONIES,

From the Earliest Time to the Present,

FORMED BY

J. HENNIKER HEATON, Esq. M.P.

INCLUDING THE FOLLOWING

Unpublished Manuscripts,

JOURNAL OF TRANSACTIONS ON NORFOLK ISLAND, by LIEUT.-GOVERNOR PHILIP GIDLEY KING, 1791-94—SIR JOS. BANKS' AUTOGRAPH UNPUBLISHED JOURNAL OF HIS VOYAGE IN THE "ENDEAVOUR" WITH CAPT. COOK, 1770 —AUTOGRAPH LETTERS AND NOTES OF GOVERNOR PHILLIP TO SIR JOS. BANKS, RELATING TO BOTANY BAY, 1787-90—TWENTY IMPORTANT AUTOGRAPH LETTERS AND NOTES BY CAPT. W. BLIGH, COMMANDER OF THE "BOUNTY," RELATING TO THE MUTINY ON BOARD THAT VESSEL.

Among the Printed Books may be mentioned the Works of :—

Angas, Barrington, Bennett, Bonwick, Buller (Birds), Curr, Dieffenbach, Dutton, Eyre, Barron Field, Flanagan, Gould (Birds of Australia, Birds of New Guinea, and Mammals of Australia), Grey, Brees, D. Collins, Capt. Cook, Matt. Flinders, Howitt, Hunter, Irwin, King, J. D. Lang, W. H. Leigh, Lycett (Views), Mitchell, Mudie, Mundy, Parkinson, Gov. Phillip, Polack, Capt. P. F. de Quir (Original Relation of Australia in Spanish, and the French and English Translations), Rusden, Seemann, Stephens, Stokes, Sturt, Sweet, Taylor, Wakefield, Wentworth, West, Westgarth, White, etc.

The Largest Collection of Scarce Pamphlets and Newspapers about Australia ever Privately Collected,

WRITINGS OF THE EARLY AUSTRALIAN POETS,

COLONIAL PARLIAMENTARY REPORTS AND TRANSACTIONS, DIRECTORIES, GUIDES, &c. &c.

Many finely Bound in Calf Gilt by Riviere.

WHICH WILL BE SOLD BY AUCTION

BY MESSRS.

SOTHEBY, WILKINSON & HODGE,

Auctioneers of Literary Property & Works illustrative of the Fine Arts,

AT THEIR HOUSE, No. 13, WELLINGTON STREET, STRAND, W.C.

On MONDAY, the 28th day of MAY, 1894, and Two Following Days, AT ONE O'CLOCK PRECISELY.

MAY BE VIEWED TWO DAYS PRIOR. CATALOGUES MAY BE HAD.

DRYDEN PRESS: J. DAVY AND SONS, 137, LONG ACRE, LONDON, W.C.

CONDITIONS OF SALE.

I. The highest bidder to be the buyer; and if any dispute arise between bidders, the lot so disputed shall be immediately put up again, provided the Auctioneer cannot decide the said dispute.

II. No person to advance less than 1s.; above five pounds, 2s. 6d.; and so on in proportion.

III. In the case of lots upon which there is a reserve, the Auctioneer shall have the right to bid on behalf of the Seller.

IV. The purchasers to give in their names and places of abode, and to pay down 10s. in the pound, if required, in part payment of the purchase-money; in default of which the lot or lots purchased to be immediately put up again and resold.

V. The lots to be taken away, at the buyer's expense, immediately after the conclusion of the sale; in default of which Messrs. SOTHEBY, WILKINSON & HODGE will not hold themselves responsible if lost, stolen, damaged, or otherwise destroyed, but they will be left at the sole risk of the purchaser. If, at the expiration of ONE WEEK after the conclusion of the sale, the books or other property are not cleared or paid for, they will then be catalogued for immediate sale, and the expense, the same as if re-sold, will be added to the amount at which the books were bought. Messrs. SOTHEBY, WILKINSON and HODGE will have the option of reselling the lots uncleared either by public or private sale without any notice being given to the defaulter.

VI. All the books are presumed to be perfect, unless otherwise expressed; but if upon collating, any should prove defective, the purchaser will be at liberty to take or reject them, provided they are returned within ONE WEEK after the conclusion of the sale, when the purchase-money will be returned.

VII. The sale of any book or books is not to be set aside on account of any worm-holes, stained or short leaves of text or plates, want of list of plates or blank leaves, or on account of the publication of any subsequent volume, supplement, appendix, or plates. All the manuscripts, autographs, all magazines and reviews, all books in lots, and all tracts in lots or volumes, will be sold with all faults, imperfections, and errors of description. The sale of any illustrated book, lot of prints or drawings is not to be set aside on account of any error in the enumeration of the numbers stated, or error of description.

VIII. No IMPERFECT BOOK will be taken back, unless a note accompanies each book, stating its imperfections, with the number of lot and date of the sale at which the same was purchased.

IX. To prevent inaccuracy in the delivery, and inconvenience in the settlement of the purchases, no lot on any account can be removed during the time of sale.

X. Upon failure of complying with the above Conditions, the money required and deposited in part of payment shall be forfeited; and *if any loss is sustained in the reselling of such lots as are not cleared or paid for, all charges on such re-sale shall be made good by the defaulters at this sale.*

Gentlemen who cannot attend the Sale may have their Commissions faithfully executed by their humble servants,

SOTHEBY, WILKINSON & HODGE,

13, Wellington Street, Strand, London.

CATALOGUE

OF THE VALUABLE

COLLECTION OF BOOKS,

Relating to Australia,

THE PROPERTY OF

J. HENNIKER HEATON, ESQ. M.P.

FIRST DAY'S SALE.

OCTAVO ET INFRA.

LOT 1.

ABORIGINES in the British Colonies (Information respecting the) Circulated by Direction of the Meeting for Sufferings, 1838—Castaway on the Auckland Isles : Narrative of the Wreck of the "Grafton," from the Journals of Capt. T. Musgrave, *map, Melbourne,* 1865 ; *all half bound*　(2)

2　"Adventure" and "Beagle." Narrative of the Surveying Voyages between 1826 and 1836 on the Southern Shores of South America, 3 vol. and Appendix to vol. II, *numerous maps and engravings, half calf*　1839

3　Alexander (Col. Sir Jas.) Incidents of the Maori War, 1860-61, *frontispiece,* 1863—Clacy (Mrs. Chas.) A Lady's Visit to the Gold Diggings, 1853—Kennedy's Colonial Travel, *n. d.*—Jung (Dr. K. E.) Australia, 1884 ; and others　(6)

4　Alexander (Major.-Gen. Sir J. E.) Bush Fighting, illustrated by Remarkable Actions and Incidents of the Maori War in New Zealand, *map, plans and woodcuts, cloth, Sampson, Low & Co.* 1873 —Palmer (Capt. Geo.) Kidnapping in the South Seas, *plates, Edinb.* 1871　(2)

5　Angas (Geo. French) Savage Life and Scenes in Australia and New Zealand, *numerous illustrations,* 2 vol. *half morocco gilt*
Smith, Elder, 1847

6 Atkinson (Jas.) Account of the State of Agriculture and Grazing in New South Wales, *coloured views and maps, half morocco*
J. Cross, 1826

7 Atkinson (Jas.) Account of the State of Agriculture and Grazing in New South Wales, *maps and coloured plates, calf gilt*
roy. 8vo. ib. 1853

8 Australasia. Stanford's Large Map, *on 4 folding sheets, in morocco case* 1859

9 Australia (The Friend of); or a Plan for exploring the interior and for carrying on a Survey of the whole Continent of Australia, by a Retired Officer, *map and coloured plates, calf gilt, m. e. by Riviere* *Hurst and Chance*, 1830

10 Australia (by G. F. Angas), *half morocco, S.P.C.K.*—Swan (N. Walter) Tales of Australian Life, *half morocco*, 1877 (2)

11 Australia, Tasmania and New Zealand (Rise and Progress of), by an Englishman, 1857—Barker (Lady) Station Life in New Zealand, 1874—Calvert (Jas.) Fiji and the Fijians, 1858—Cheever (Rev. H. T.) Life in the Sandwich Islands, *frontispiece*, 1851 ; and others (7)

12 Australian Almanack and General Directory for 1835, by E. W. O'Shaughnessey *Sydney*

13 Australian Medical Journal (The) edited under the Superintendence of the Medical Society of Victoria, from Jan. 1861 to Dec. 1880, 20 vol. *half bound (not uniform), (sold with all faults), Melbourne*

14 Australian Tales, by Old Boomerang 1868

15 Australian (The) a Monthly Magazine, *plates*, vol. I-V, *cloth*, *Sydney*, Oct. 1878-Dec. 1880—Australian Home Companion, vol. IV, V and VI *(no title to vol. VI)*, *cloth, ib.* 1859-61 (8)

16 Australian Temperance Magazine, vol. I, *Sydney*, 1838—Allwood (Rev. R.) Lectures on the Papal Claim of Jurisdiction, *ib.* 1843 —Allen (D.) History of the Convent, *ib.* 1878 ; &c. (16)

17 Australian Handbook and Almanac, etc. (The) for 1871-3, 1877, 1881, 1883, 1884, 1886, 1887 and 1891, 10 vol.—Year Book of Australia, 1888-92, 4 vol.—Official Directory and Almanack of Australia, 1883, *bound in Australian morocco*, and 1884, *half morocco* (16)

18 Australian Sporting Celebrities, with Biographical Sketches by "Vigilant," *woodcut portraits, Melbourne*, 1887 — Victorian Stud Book, vol. II *(title torn), ib.* 1865—Curr (E. M.) Pure Saddle-Horses, and how to Breed them in Australia *(lower margins slightly damaged), ib.* 1863 — Australian Turf Guide, 1878, *Sydney*, 1879 (4)

19 Australian Pocket Almanack for the Year 1825, published under the Sanction of his Excellency Sir Thos. Brisbane, *half morocco*, VERY RARE *Australia, R. Howe*, 1825

20 Australian Cricketers' Tour through Australia, New Zealand, and Great Britain, by Argus, *Sydney*, 1878—Conway's Australian Cricketers' Annual for 1876-7, *Melbourne*—The Footballer in Victoria, edited by T. P. Power, *ib.* 1876—English and Australian Cookery Book, 1864—History of the First Bushmen's Club in S. Australia, *Adelaide*, 1872 ; and others (8)

21 Australian Directory, vol. I (*all published*), 1830—M'Douall Stuart's
Explorations across the Continent of Australia, *Melbourne*,
1863—Journal of Landsborough's Expedition from Carpentaria
in Search of Burke and Wills, *ib.* 1862—Report of the Select
Committee of the House of Commons on Transportation,
1838—Earl (G. Windsor) Handbook for Colonists in Tropical
Australia, 1882 ; and others   (16)
22 Australian Monthly Magazine, vol. I, III, IV, and various Nos.—
Various Parts of Colonial Magazines, etc.   *a parcel*
23 Australian Freemasons' Magazine (The), vol. I, *Sydney*, 1870—
Barton (G. B.) Poets and Prose Writers of New South Wales,
ib. 1866 — Australian Monthly Magazine for 1866, *half
morocco* — Gill (T.) Bibliography of South Australia, *half
morocco*, 1885 ; and others   (7)
24 Australian Celebrities, &c. Personal Portraits of 100 Theatrical
Stars of Various Magnitudes, *printed in script type, Melbourne,
H. T. Dwight*, 1865—Fox (W.) The Six Colonies of New
Zealand, *map*, 1851—Clutterbuck (Dr.) Port Phillip in 1849 ;
and others   (13)
25 AUSTRALIAN PAMPHLETS. A Collection of Pamphlets relating
to the various Australian Colonies, including Early Poetry,
Guides, Local Printing, Local Topography, Popular Songs,
Privately Printed Tracts, Gold and Gold Mining, Theo-
logy, Tales and Sketches, Agriculture, Statistics, Trials,
Almanacks and Directories, Aborigines, Wine-Growing, etc.
etc. *many very scarce, some with maps and illustrations*, in 51 vol.
half morocco   *v. d.*
26 Australian Pamphlets. Another Scarce Collection, in 22 vol. *cloth*
                                                               v. d.
27 Australian Pamphlets. Mueller (F.) Fragmenta Phytographiæ
Australiæ, vol. I, *Melbourne*, 1858-9—Shepherd (T. W.)
Catalogue of Plants cultivated at the Darling Nursery, *Sidney*,
1851—Magnetic Observations, *Melbourne*, 1857—Instructions
for the Guidance of Meteorological Observers in Victoria, 1857
—Brown (R.) Botanical Appendix to Capt. Sturt's Expedition
into Central Australia, *n. d.*—Mueller, Definitions of hitherto
Undescribed Australian Plants, *Melbourne*, 1855—Lang (J. D.)
Cooksland or the Moreton Bay District of New South Wales,
1848—The Emigrant's Guide to California, *maps and illustrations, n. d.* ; and others, in 4 vol. *some scarce*   *v. d.*
28 Australian Pamphlets. New Zealand, Tasmania, 1855-63, Victoria,
(1855-72), New South Wales, &c. *some scarce*, bound in 8 vol. *v.d.*
29 AUSTRALIAN POETS AND POETRY. A'Beckett (Sir Wm. *Chief
Justice of Victoria*) The Earl's Choice, and other Poems, 1863—
Le Gay Brereton (J.) Travels of Prince Legion, and Poems,
2 vol. 1857-65—Leakey (Caroline W.) Lyra Australis, 1854—
Wilson (Mrs. R.) New Zealand, and other Poems, 1851 ; and
another   (6)
30 Australian Poets, etc. Balance of Pain (The) and other Poems,
by Australie, *G. Bell*, 1877 — Sinclair (Fr.) Ballads and
Poems from the Pacific, 1889—Sharp (Wm.) Earth's Voices,
Transcripts from Nature, etc. 1884—Sherard (C. A.) A
Daughter of the South, etc. 1889—Le Gay Brereton (J.)
Poems, 1865 ; and another   (6)

31   Australian Poets, etc. Corbyn (C. A.) Sydney Revels of Bacchus, Cupid and Momus, *Sydney, Hawkesley & Williamson*, 1854—Michael (Jas. L.) Songs without Music, and John Cumberland (a Poem), 2 vol. *Sydney*, 1857—Flanagan (R. J.) Australian and other Poems, *ib.* 1887—Holdsworth (P. J.) Station Hunting on the Warrego, etc. *ib.* 1885 ; and others   (13)

32   Australian Poets, etc. Crinoliniad, an Epic Poem, by D. P. C. *half bound, West Maitland*, 1867—Mair (Chas.) Dreamland and other Poems, *Montreal, n. d.*—McCrae (G. Gordon) Māmba ("The Bright Eyed"), *Melbourne*, 1867—Gordon (A. L.) Ashtaroth ; a Dramatic Lyric, *ib.* 1867 ; &c.   (9)

33   Australian Poets, etc. Goodrich (Newton) Poetical Work, *half bound, Melbourne, G. Robertson*, 1873—Capper (R.) Dramatic Illustrations of Ancient History, *ib.* 1868—Sutherland (Alex.) Thirty Short Poems, *Melville, Mullen & Slade*, 1890—Simmonds (Jas.) *Comedian*, Lyrics, *Sydney*, 1858—Wilson (J. Sydney) Australian Poems and Songs, *ib.* 1870 ; and others (10)

34   Australian Poets, etc. Harpur (Ch.) Poems, *Melbourne, G. Robertson*, 1883—Whiteman (John) Sparks and Sounds from a Colonial Anvil, *ib.* 1873—Capper (R.) Dramatic Illustrations of Ancient History, *ib.* 1868—The Golden Spring, etc. by J. Owen Tucker, *ib.* 1865 ; and others   (12)

35   Australian Poets. Horne (R. Hengist). Orion (*Farthing Edition*), 1843—The same (*Australian Edition*), *Melbourne*, 1854—Ballad Romances, *Ch. Ollier*, 1846—Prometheus the Fire-bringer (*Australian Edition*), *Melbourne*, 1866—The Great Peacemaker, *Lond.* (*Privately Printed*), 1872 ; and another   (5)

36   Australian Poets. Kendall (Henry). Poems and Songs, FIRST EDITION, *very scarce, half bound, Sydney, J. R. Clarke*, 1862—Leaves from Australian Forests, FIRST EDITION, *cloth, Melbourne, G. Robertson*, 1869—Songs from the Mountains, *cloth,* (*with Autograph Letter*), *Sydney and London*, 1880   (3)

37   Australian Poets. Knox (J.) Poetic Trifles, *half calf, very scarce*
        Hobart Town, S.A. Tegg, 1838

*** The first volume of Poetry published in Tasmania, dedicated to Sir John Franklin.

38   Australian Poets, etc. Lang (Dr. J. Dunmore) Aurora Australis, or Specimens of Sacred Poetry for the Colonists of Australia, *half calf, very scarce*   *Sydney, G. Eagar,* 1826

39   Australian Poets, etc. Leakey (Caroline W.) Lyra Australis, or Attempts to Sing in a Strange Land, *half morocco*, 1854—Wilson (Mrs. Rob.) New Zealand, and other Poems, 1851—Broome (F. N.) Poems from New Zealand, 1868—Hervey (T. K.) Australian and other Poems, 1825—Ollivant (J. E.) Hine Moa, the Maori Maiden, *n. d.*—Sinclair (Jas.) Australian Sacred Lyre, *Melbourne*, 1857   (6)

40   Australian Poets. Meredith (Mrs.) Romance of Nature, *coloured plates of flowers, Tilt*, 1839—The Southern Chimes, Hymns and Tunes for Australia, *Castlemaine*, 1870—Grandmamma's Verse Book, by Mrs. Meredith, *Tasmania*, 1878; &c.   (9)

41 Australian Poets, etc. Moore (J. Sheridan) Spring-Life Lyrics, *sheep, Sydney, Reading & Wellbank*, 1864—Gordon (J. *of New South Wales*) Botany Bay, and other Poems, 1861—Forster (W.) The Weir Wolf, 1876—Hervey (T. K.) Australia and other Poems, 1824—Cambridge Prize Poems (Australasia, by W. M. Praed, etc.) *calf*, 1828 ; and 1 other (6)

42 Australian Poets. Parkes (Sir Henry). Murmurs of the Stream, *Sydney, J. W. Waugh*, 1857—The Beauteous Terrorist and other Poems, by a Wanderer (Sir H. Parkes), *Melbourne*, 1885 —Fragmentary Thoughts, *Sydney*, 1889 (3)

43 Australian Poets. Rae (John) Gleanings from My Scrapbook *Sydney, printed by the Author*, 1869

44 Australian Poets. Russell (Dr. Alex. *Dean of Adelaide*) The Seeker and other Poems, *Adelaide*, 1881—Bruce (Robert, *of Wallelberdina, S. A.*) A Voice from the Australian Bush, *plates, ib*. 1877—Poems by Austral, *ib*. 1873—Isaacs (G.) Not for Sale, a Selection of Imaginative Pieces, *ib*. 1869—Chandler (A. T.) A Bush Idyl, and other Poems, *ib*. 1886—Richards (W. P.) Poems, etc. *ib*. 1881 (6)

45 Australian Poets, etc. Sladen (Douglas W. B.). Australian Poets, 1788-1888, *cloth*, 1888—In Cornwall, and Across the Sea, etc. 1885—Australian Lyrics, *second edition, presentation copy*, 1885—Selected Australian Ballads, 1888—A Poetry of Exiles, *Sydney, C. E. Fuller*, 1883 (5)

46 Australian Poets, etc. Sladen. A Century of Australian Song, 1888—In Cornwall and across the Sea, 1885—Australian Lyrics, *Melbourne, G. Robertson*, 1883—A Summer Christmas, *n. d.*—Frithjof and Ingebjorg, 1882 (5)

47 Australian Poets. Stephens (J. Brunton) Miscellaneous Poems, *Brisbane*, 1880—Marsupial Bill (by the same), *woodcut, ib*. 1879—Cameron (Rev. C. Innes) Poems and Hymns, *Geelong*, 1870—Westerley Busters, by D. Mayne, *Bathurst, D. Mayne*, 1879—Bracken (Thos.) Flowers of the Free Lands (*wants title*), *Dunedin*, 1877 (5)

48 Authentic Narrative of four Years Residence at Tongataboo, *frontispiece*, 1810—Journal of Landsborough's Expedition from Carpentaria in search of Burke and Wills, *map, Melbourne*, 1862—Lang (J. D.) New Zealand in 1839 ; and others, *all half bound* (5)

49 Backhouse (Jas.) Narrative of a Visit to the Australian Colonies, *maps, etchings and woodcuts, calf extra by Riviere Hamilton & Co*. 1843

50 Backhouse (Jas.) Narrative of a Visit to the Australian Colonies, and to the Mauritius and South Africa, 2 vol. *maps and illustrations, cloth* 1843-4

51 Baden-Powell (Geo. S.) New Homes for the Old Country (Australia and New Zealand), *numerous illustrations, cloth gilt R. Bentley*, 1872

52 Bailliere's Tasmanian Gazetteer, *map, Hobart Town*, 1877—New South Wales Gazetteer, *map, Sydney*, 1866—South Australian Gazetteer, *map, Adelaide*, 1866—New South Wales in 1881, by T. Richards, *Sydney*, 1882 ; and others (9)

53   Baker (Ch. John) Sydney and Melbourne, with the present State and future prospects of New S. Wales, *map, half bound*, 1845—Binney (T.) Church Life in Australia, 1860—Fox (Lady Mary) Account of an Expedition to the Interior of New Holland, 1837—Matthew (P.) Emigration Fields, North America, the Cape, Australia and New Zealand, 1839   (4)

54   Baker (C. J.) Sydney and Melbourne, and the Present State and Future Prospects of New South Wales, *map, calf gilt, Smith, Elder*, 1845—Griffith (Chas.) Present State and Prospects of Port Phillip District of New South Wales, *frontispiece, calf gilt, Dublin, Curry*, 1845   (2)

55   Barrington (Geo. *Superintendent of the Convicts at Paramatta*) Voyage to New South Wales, 1795—Sequel to the Voyage to New South Wales, 1800—Memoirs of George Barrington from his birth to his Conviction at the Old Bailey, 1790 ; in 1 vol. *calf extra, m. e.*

56   Barrington (Geo.) Voyage to Botany Bay (with the Sequel), *some leaves soiled and slightly mended, half morocco*
                12mo. *C. Lowndes for H. D. Symonds* (1801)

57   Barrington (Geo.) History of New South Wales, Botany Bay, Port Jackson, &c. *coloured plates, old red morocco*   *M. Jones*, 1802

58   Barrington (Geo.) History of New South Wales. Another copy, *calf*   1802

59   Barrington (Geo.) Account of a Voyage to New South Wales, with his Life, Trials, Speeches, &c. *portrait and coloured plates, calf gilt, m. e. by Riviere*   *M. Jones*, 1810

60   Barrington (Geo.) Memoirs, from his birth in 1755 to his last Conviction at the Old Bailey, Sept. 17, 1790, *frontispiece, half bound, M. Smith*, 1790—Barrington's Voyage to New South Wales, *chapbook edition, half bound, printed by A. Swindells, Hanging Bridge, Manchester, n. d.*   (2)

61   Barsanti (P. Ott.) I Selvaggi dell' Australia   *Roma*, 1868

62   Barton (G. B.) Literature in New South Wales, and the Poets and Prose Writers of New South Wales, 2 vol.   *Sydney*, 1866

63   Barton (G. B.) Poets and Prose Writers of New South Wales, *Sydney*, 1866—View of the Art of Civilization, edited by E. G. Wakefield, 1849—Wreck of the "Favourite" on the Island of Desolation, *map and cuts*, 1850   (3)

64   Barton (G. B.) Literature in New South Wales, *Sydney*, 1866—Caldwell (R.) The Gold Era of California, *map*, 1855 ; &c. (4)

65   Barton (G. B.) History of New South Wales from the Records, vol. I (Governor Phillip, 1783-9), *cloth*
             Sydney, C. Potter, 1889

66   Baudoin (A.) L'Aventure de Port Breton, *half morocco, Paris, M. Dreyfous, s. d.*—De Beauvoir (Comte de) Australie, Voyage autour du Monde, *maps and illustrations, Paris, Plon*, 1871—D'Albertis, La Nouvelle Guinée, *ib. Hachette*, 1883—Perron d'Arc, Aventures d'un Voyageur en Australie, *ib.* 1879 ; and others   (10)

67 Beaney (J. G.) Constitutional Syphilis, 20 *coloured plates (top of title cut)*, *Melbourne*, 1872—Syphilis, its Nature and Diffusion Popularly Considered, 15 *coloured plates, ib.* 1869—Thomson (Wm.) On Typhoid Fever, *imp. 8vo, ib.* 1874 (3)

68 Bennett (Geo.) Wanderings in New South Wales, &c. 1832-34, 2 vol. *frontispieces and woodcuts, tree-calf gilt, m. e. by Riviere*
Bentley, 1834

69 Bennett (Geo.) Another copy, 2 vol. *plates, half bound* *ib.* 1834

70 Bennett (Geo.) Gatherings of a Naturalist in Australasia, *coloured plates, Van Voorst*, 1860—Woods (Rev. J. E.) Geological Observations in South Australia, *plates*, 1862—Scoresby (Rev. W.) Voyage to Australia and Round the World for Magnetic Research, *portrait*, 1859 (3)

71 Bennett (Sam.) History of Australian Discovery and Colonisation, *plates, tinted, red morocco extra, g. e. very scarce*
Sydney, Hanson & Bennett, 1867

72 Bennet (R. G.) Verhandeling, over de Nederlandsche Ontdekkingen in Amerika, Australië, de Indiën, &c. *with folio atlas of maps in a roll, Utrecht*, 1827—Twee Togten naar de Golf Van Carpentaria (J. Cartensz, 1623, J. E. Gonzal, 1756), *Amst. J. H. Scheltema*, 1859 ; and others (6)

73 Betach (Wm.) Voyage Round the World in the year 1719 to Cruise on the Spaniards in the Great South Ocean, *old calf*, 1728—Voyage to the Isle of Mauritius by a French Officer, translated by John Parish, 1775 (2)

74 Bidwill (J. Carne) Rambles in New Zealand, *map*, 1841—Brodie (W.) Remarks on the Past and Present State of New Zealand, 1845—Savage (John) Some Account of New Zealand, *plate*, 1807 ; in 1 vol. *tree-calf extra, m. e. by Riviere*

75 Bingle (John, *of New South Wales*) Letter to Lord Glenelg (on his Trial for Felonry), *very rare* 1837

76 Bischoff (Jas.) Sketch of the History of Van Diemen's Land, with an Account of the Van Diemen's Land Co. *plates and map, tree-calf extra, m. e. by Riviere* *J. Richardson*, 1832

77 Bond (G.) Brief Account of the Colony of Port Jackson, 1803—Narrative of the Sufferings of T. F. Palmer and W. Skirving during a Voyage to New South Wales, 1794, *Camb.* 1797 (2)

78 Bonwick (Jas.) Various Writings, viz. : Port Phillip, *Melbourne*, 1856—Astronomy for Young Australians, *ib.* 1864—Reader for Australian Youth, *Adelaide*, 1852—Western Victoria in 1857, *Geelong*—John Batman, *Melbourne*, 1867—Notes of a Gold Digger, *ib.* 1852—Early Days of Melbourne, 1857—Resources of Queensland, 1883 (8)

79 Bonwick (Jas.) Various Writings, viz. : Romance of the Wool Trade, 1887—Wild White Man and the Blacks of Victoria, *Melbourne*, 1863—Western Australia, 1885—Discovery and Settlement of Port Phillip, *Melbourne*, 1856—Resources of Queensland, *map*, 1883—Grammar for Australian Youth, *Adelaide*, 1851—The Bushrangers, *Melbourne*, 1856—Geography of Australia and New Zealand, *ib.* 1855—John Batman, the founder of Victoria, *ib.* 1868—Astronomy for Young Australians, *ib.* 1864 ; and Early Days of Melbourne, *ib.* 1857 (11)

80   Bonwick (Jas.) Daily Life and Origin of the Tasmanians, *plates,
     cloth,* 1870—Turner (Rev. G.) Nineteen Years in Polynesia,
     illustrations, 1861—Speeches of Sir Hercules Robinson, *portrait,
     Sydney,* 1879—Barton (G. W.) Poets and Prose Writers of
     New South Wales, *ib.* 1866   (4)
81   Bonwick (Jas.) The Last of the Tasmanians, *numerous illustrations
     (some coloured), cloth,* 1870—Sidney (S.) Three Colonies of
     Australia, *woodcuts, cloth,* 1852—Terry (Ch.) New Zealand as
     a British Colony, *plates (wants map),* 1842   (3)
82   Bonwick (James). Last of the Tasmanians, *coloured and other illus-
     trations,* 1870—Egyptian Belief and Modern Thought, *front.*
     1878—The Tasmanian Lily, 1873—Romance of the Wool
     Trade (*autograph letter inserted*), 1887—The Lost Tasmanian
     Race, 1884   (5)
83   Bonwick (James) Port Phillip Settlement, *map, plates and facsimiles
     (autograph letters of the author), cloth*   S. Low, 1873
84   Bonwick (James). Discovery and Settlement of Port Phillip, *map,
     Melbourne,* 1856—Early Struggles of the Australian Press,
     1890—John Batman, Founder of Victoria, *Melbourne,* 1867—
     The Bushrangers, *ib.* 1856—Wesleyan Methodism in South
     Australia, *Adelaide, n. d.;* and other small books by the
     same   (9)
85   Bowman (Hildebrand) Travels into Carnovirria, Taupiniera, Olfac-
     taria and Auditante, in New Zealand, in the Island of Bon-
     hommica, &c. (*satirical*), *calf*   W. Strahan, 1778
86   Brady (Very Rev. J.) Descriptive Vocabulary of the Native
     Language of W. Australia   Rome, 1845
87   Braim (T. H.) New Homes: Australian Colonies and New Zea-
     land, *illustrated,* 1870—Gane (D. M.) New South Wales and
     Victoria in 1885, 1886—Social Life and Manners in Australia
     by an eight years' Resident, 1861—Swainson (Wm.) New
     Zealand and the War, 1862; and others   (6)
88   Brees (S. C.) Guide and Description of the Panorama of New
     Zealand, *plates, n. d.*—Prout (J. G.) Illustrated Handbook to
     the Voyage to Australia, *n. d.*—Cook (S.) Prize Essay on the
     Future Land Policy of New South Wales, *Sydney,* 1870—
     North Western Australia, its Soil, Climate, &c. *map, Melbourne,*
     1864—McCombie (Hon. T.) Frank Henly, or Honesty will
     Conquer, *ib.* 1867   (5)
89   Breton (Lieut.) Excursions in New South Wales, Western Aus-
     tralia and Van Diemen's Land, 1830-33, *frontispiece, half
     morocco,* 1833—Wells (B.) History of Taranaki, *frontispiece,
     New Zealand,* 1878; and others   (6)
90   Breton (Lieut.) Excursions in New South Wales, Western Aus-
     tralia and Van Diemen's Land, 1830-33, *second edition, frontis-
     piece, half calf,* 1834—Landor (E. W.) The Bushman, or Life
     in a New Country, *plates, half calf,* 1847   (2)
91   Brown (Henry) Victoria as I found it during Five Years of
     Adventure, 1862—Cholmondeley (Thos.) Ultima Thule, or
     Thoughts on New Zealand, *J. Chapman,* 1854—Wilkins (W.)
     Australasia, 1888—Williams (John) Missionary Enterprises
     in the South Sea Islands, *woodcuts,* 1838; and others   (8)

92 Brown (Rob.) Miscellaneous Botanical Works, 2 vol. *cloth (and 4to atlas of plates)* *Ray Society*, 1866-7-8

93 Brown. Another copy, 2 vol. *(and 4to atlas of plates) ib.* 1866-7-8

94 Brown (Capt. Thos.) Manual of the New Zealand Colœoptera, *half morocco* *imp. 8vo. Wellington, J. Hughes*, 1880

95 Brown (Rev. Wm.) History of Christian Missions, 3 vol. *third edition, cloth, T. Baker*, 1864—Tyermann and Bennett. Journal of Voyages and Travels, compiled by Jas. Montgomery, 2 vol. *portraits and plates, half calf,* 1831 (5)

96 Brown (Wm.) New Zealand and its Aborigines, *tree-calf extra, m. e. by Rivière* *Smith Elder*, 1845

97 Brown (Wm.) New Zealand and its Aborigines, 1851—Train (G. J.) The Merchant abroad in Europe, Asia and Australia, 1857—Adams (C. W. A.) A Spring in the Canterbury Settlement, *plates*, 1853—British Colonisation of New Zealand, *illustrated*, 1837 ; and others (7)

98 Brown (Wm.) New Zealand and its Aborigines, 1845—Musgrave (Capt. T.) Castaway on the Auckland Islands, 1806—Horne (R. H.) Australian Facts and Prospects, 1859—Wight (George) Queensland for British Labour, *map, n. d. ;* and others (6)

99 Brougham (Lord) An Inquiry into the Colonial Policy of the European Nations, 2 vol. *half morocco, uncut* *Edinb.* 1803

100 Buchanan (John) Manual of the Indigenous Grasses of New Zealand, 57 *plates, half morocco* *imp. 8vo. Wellington, J. Hughes*, 1880

101 Buller (W. L.) Manual of the Birds of New Zealand, 37 *plates and woodcuts, cloth* *New Zealand*, 1882

102 Burn (David) Plays and Fugitive Pieces in Verse, 2 vol. in 1, *cloth, uncut* *Hobart Town, V.D.L. W. Pratt*, 1842

103 Burns. Another copy, 2 vol. in 1, *boards, uncut* *ib.* 1842

104 Burton (Judge W. W.) State of Religion and Education in New South Wales, *map, calf gilt, y. e.* *J. Cross*, 1840

105 Burton. Religion in New South Wales, 1840—Sidney (S.) Gallops and Gossips in the Bush of Australia, 1854—The Prisoners of Australia, a Narrative, 1841—Jordan (J. C.) Management of Sheep and Stations, *Melbourne*, 1867 ; *all half bound* (4)

106 Burton (Judge W. W.) State of Religion and Education in New South Wales, *map*, 1840—Lang (J. D.) Freedom and Independence for the United Provinces of Australia, *map*, 1870—Victoria, Report of the Debates in both Houses of Parliament on Reform of the Constitution, Session 1878, *Melbourne ;* and others (6)

107 Busby (Jas.) Manual of Plain Directions for Planting and Cultivating Vineyards and for Making Wine in New South Wales *Sydney, R. Mansfield*, 1830

108 Busby (Jas.) Our Colonial Empire and the Case of New Zealand, *Williams & Norgate, n. d.*—Parker (Capt. John) Voyage Round the World in the Gorgon Man of War, 1795—Irwin (Capt. J. C.) State and Position of Western Australia, 1835 —Jeffreys (Lieut. Ch.) Van Diemen's Land, 1820 ; &c. (5)

109 Busby (Jas.) Authentic Information relative to New South Wales and New Zealand, *map* 1832

110 Busby (Jas.) Authentic Information relative to New South Wales and New Zealand 1832

111 Byrne (J. C.) Twelve Years' Wanderings in the British Colonies, 1835-47, 2 vol. *map, cloth, R. Bentley*, 1848—Millett (Mrs. E.) An Australian Parsonage, *frontispiece, E. Stanford*, 1872 (3)

112 Campbell (Dr. T.) Diary of a Visit to England in 1775, with Notes by S. Raymond, *very rare* *Sydney*, 1854

113 Capital Punishment Commission (Report of the) with Minutes of Evidence, *imp. 8vo. Sydney, T. Richards*, 1868—Report on the Common School System of the United States, 2 *copies, ib.* 1868—Handbook to the Customs, Laws and Practice of New South Wales, *ib.* 1882 ; and another (5)

114 Carron (Wm.) Narrative of an Expedition for the Exploration of Rockingham Bay and Cape York, *map* *Sydney*, 1849

115 Castella (H. de) John Bull's Vineyard, Australian Sketches *Australia*, 1886

116 Catalogue of the Melbourne Public Library, *morocco*, 1861— Catalogue of the Library of the Royal Colonial Institute, 1886—Catalogue of the York Gate Library—Denmark Delineated, part I, *plates ;* and others (10)

117 Chamerovzow (L. A.) The New Zealand Question and the Rights of Aborigines, *a limited number printed, calf gilt, by Rivière* *T. C. Newby*, 1848

118 Chamerovzow (L. A.) The New Zealand Question and the Rights of Aborigines, 1848—Maconochie(Capt.) Australiana, Thoughts on Convict Management, &c. *Parker*, 1839—Bischoff (Jas.) Sketch of the History of Van Diemen's Land, *plates (wants map)*, 1832—Howell (Mrs. W. May) Reminiscences of Australia, The Diggings and the Bush, *privately printed*, 1869 ; and others (6)

119 Cholmondeley (Thos.) Ultima Thule ; Thoughts suggested by a Residence in New Zealand, *half morocco*, 1854—Melville (H.) Omoo : Narrative of Adventures in the South Seas, 1847— Bunce (D.) Australiatic Reminiscences, *portrait, half bound, Melbourne*, 1857—Capper (H.) South Australia, 3 *maps*, 1839; and others (7)

120 Christmann (Fr.) Australien, *numerous illustrations, two editions, Leipz.* 1870-80—Jung (Dr. K. E.) Der Welttheil Australien, 4 vol. *numerous illustrations, ib.* 1882—Um die Welt Ohne zu Wollen, 100 *illustrations, Würzburg*, 1883 ; and others (8)

121 Clacy (Mrs. Ch.) Lights and Shadows of Australian Life, 2 vol. *cloth* *Hurst and Blackett*, 1854

122 Clarke (Rev. W. B.) Remarks on the Sedimentary Formations of New South Wales, *plans, half bound, Sydney*, 1878—Daintree (R.) Notes on the Geology of the Colony of Queensland, 1872—Catalogue of the Land Mollusca of New Zealand, 1873 —Buller (W.) On the New Zealand Bat (Trans. N. Z. Institute), 1870—Scott (A. W.) Mammalia recent and extinct, *Sydney*, 1873—Gould (John) Introduction to the Mammals of Australia, 1863 (6)

123 Clarke (Rev. W. B.) Researches in the Southern Gold Fields of New South Wales, *map, Sydney,* 1860—Statistical View of Van Diemen's Land, *map,* 1832—Journal of J. G. Macdonald to Carpentaria and back, *portrait, Brisbane,* 1865—McFarland (A.) Illawarra and Manaro, *Sydney,* 1872 ; and others (7)

124 Clarke (Rev. W. B.) Researches in the Southern Gold Fields of New South Wales, *map, Sydney,* 1860—Busby (Jas.) The Australian Farmer and Land Owner's Guide, 1839—Hargraves (E. H.) Australia and its Gold Fields, *map,* 1855—Curr (E.) Account of the Colony of Van Diemen's Land, 1824 ; and others (6)

125 Clarke. Long Odds, a Novel, by Marcus Clarke, *illustrated Melbourne,* 1869

125* Cobbold (Rev. R.) Margaret Catchpole, 3 vol. *plates, cloth* 1845

126 Coghlan (T. A.) Wealth and Progress of New South Wales, 1886-7, *cloth, Sydney,* 1887—Hingston (Jas.) The Australian Abroad, 1879—Kothari Jehangir (H.) Impressions of a first Tour Round the World, *privately printed,* 1889 (3)

127 Colonial Year Book, 1890-91, 2 vol.—Sell's Directory of Registered Telegraphic Addresses, 1890 — Canada Statistical Record, 1888 ; Canadian Handbook, 1886 ; and others (10)

128 Comic History (The) of New South Wales, by H. N. Montagu, *illustrated, no title* (1882)

129 Comments on Convict Discipline of New South Wales *Sydney,* 1834

130 Cooper (Ellwood) Forest Culture and Eucalyptus Trees, *half morocco, San Francisco,* 1876—Victoria Gold Valuer's Ready Reckoner and Assayer's Chemical Guide, 1853—Russell (A.) Tour through the Australian Colonies, 1840 ; and others (5)

131 Cooper (H. Stonehewer) Coral Lands, 2 vol. *photos, cloth, Bentley,* 1880—Coote (Walter) Wanderings South and East, *maps and illustrations, cloth, S. Low,* 1882—Prout (Ebenezer) Life of the Rev. John Williams, 1843 (4)

132 Cooper (F. de Brébant) Wild Adventures in Australia and New South Wales, 1857—Landsborough's Exploration, edited by J. G. Laurie, *n. d.*—Atkins (Rev. T.) Wanderings of the Clerical Eulysses in Tasmania, 1859—Swainson's New Zealand, 1856 ; and others (9)

133 Crawford (J. C.) Recollections of Travel in New Zealand and Australia, *maps and illustrations, cloth,* 1880—Seemann (B.) Viti, 1860-1, *map and illustrations, cloth,* 1862 — Old New Zealand by a Pakeha Maori, *cloth,* 1876 (3)

134 Cruise (Maj. R. A.) Journal of a ten months Residence in New Zealand, *second edition, tree-calf extra, m. e. by Riviere Longmans,* 1824

135 Cruise (R. A.) Journal of a Ten Months' Residence in New Zealand, *frontispiece, calf* 1824

136 Cumming (C. F. Gordon) A Lady's Cruise in a French Man of War, 2 vol. *maps and plates, cloth* *Blackwood,* 1882

12

137 Cunningham (P.) Two Years in New South Wales, 2 vol. *tree-calf gilt, m. e. by Riviere, H. Colburn*, 1827—Backhouse (J.) Extracts from Letters from Van Diemen's Land, New South Wales, &c. 2 vol. *calf gilt by Rivière*, 1842 (4)

138 Cunningham (P.) Two Years in New South Wales, *second edition*, 2 vol. *map*, 1827—Russell (A.) Tour through the Australian Colonies in 1839, *Glasgow*, 1840—Busby (Jas.) Culture of the Vine in New South Wales, 1840 ; and others (8)

139 Curiosities of Entomology, *coloured plates, Groombridge, n. d.*— Henniker (J.) Two Letters on the Origin, Antiquity and History of Norman Tiles, with Armorial Bearings, *plates, half bound*, 1794—Duffy (Sir C. Gavan) League of North and South, 1886—Defoe's Roxana and Mother Ross, *Bohn*, 1855 ; and others (8)

140 Curr (Edw.) An Account of the Colony of Van Diemen's Land, *calf gilt, G. Cowie*, 1824—Earl (G. Windsor) Enterprise in Tropical Australia, *maps, tree-calf gilt, Madden*, 1846 — Fox (Lady Mary) Account of an Expedition to the Interior of New Holland, *tree-calf gilt, R. Bentley*, 1837 (3)

141 CURR (EDW. M.) THE AUSTRALIAN RACE, its Origin, Languages, Customs, &c. 4 vol. (*vol. IV, folio ; Comparative Vocabulary*), *cloth*   *Melbourne, J. Ferres*, 1886-7

142 Curtis (John) Shipwreck of the Stirling Castle and the Charles Eaton, *plates, Virtue*, 1838—Lang (J. D.) The Convict's Bank, *Sydney*, 1855—National Education, *Melbourne, " Argus " Office*, 1853—Bland (W.) Letters from the Australian Patriotic Association to Ch. Buller, M.P. *Sydney*, 1849 ; &c. (13)

143 D'Albertis (L. M.) New Guinea : What I did and What I saw, 2 vol. *numerous illustrations, those of Natural History coloured, cloth*   *Sampson Low*, 1880

144 Dampier. A Collection of Voyages, by Dampier, Wafer, Cowley, Sharp, Wood, Roberts, &c. 4 vol. *numerous maps and plates, old calf, J. Knapton*, 1729 ; and 2 others (6)

145 Dampier (Guill.) Nouveau Voyage autour du Monde, 5 vol. *maps and plates, old calf*   *Rouen, R. Machuel*, 1715

146 Darwin (Ch.) Descent of Man, 1874—Jones (T. R.) Mammalia, *illustrated, Warne*—Wilson (Sir S.) Salmon at the Antipodes, 1879—Quaife (B.) The Intellectual Sciences, 2 vol. *Sydney, n. d. ;* and others (7)

147 Davison (Simpson) Discovery and Geognosy of Gold Deposits in Australia, *map*, 1860—Dutton (Fr.) South Australia and its Mines, &c. *plates*, 1846—Moore (C. Fl.) Diary of an early Settler in Western Australia, with a Vocabulary of the Language of the Aborigines, 1884 (3)

148 Dawson (Rob.) Present State of Australia, *second edition, half morocco*   *Smith, Elder*, 1831

149 Dawson (Rob.) Present State of Australia, with Reference to Emigration, *second edition, calf gilt, Smith, Elder*, 1831—Sidney (S.) Three Colonies of Australia, *numerous woodcuts (no map), calf gilt, Cooke*, 1852 (2)

150 Dawson (R.) Present State of Australia, 1831—Sidney (S.) Three Colonies of Australia, *map and woodcuts*, 1853—Lyne (Ch.) Industries of New South Wales, 1882—Coghlan (T. A.) Wealth and Progress of New South Wales, 1889-90 ; &c. (5)

150* De Boos. Fifty Years ago, an Australian Tale, by Ch. de Boos, *Sydney*, 1867 ; and others (4)

151 De Laborde. Histoire Abrégé de la Mer du Sud, 3 vol. *calf, Paris, Didot*, 1791—De Rienzi (G. L. Domeny) Océanie, ou Cinquième partie du Monde, 3 vol. *numerous illustrations, half bound, ib.* 1836 (6)

152 Denison (Sir Wm.) Varieties of Vice-Regal Life, 2 vol. *maps of Tasmania, &c. half calf gilt* Longmans, 1870

153 D'Estrey (Comte Meyners) La Paponasie, ou Nouvelle-Guinée Occidentale, *map and plates, half morocco imp. 8vo. Paris,* 1881

154 Dickinson (Jas.) The Wreath, a Gardener's Manual, arranged for the Climate of Tasmania, *portrait, Tasmania,* 1855—Earl (G. W.) Handbook for Colonists in Tropical Australia, *Penang,* 1863, *Lond.* 1882 ; and others (4)

155 Dieffenbach (Dr. Ern.) Travels in New Zealand, with contributions to the Geography, Geology, Botany and Natural History of that Country, *plates,* 2 vol. *tree-calf extra, m. e. by Rivière*
J. Murray, 1843

156 Dieffenbach. Travels in New Zealand. Another copy, *frontispieces,* 2 vol. *green cloth* ib. 1843

157 Dilke (Sir C. W.) Greater Britain, *maps and illustrations,* 2 vol. *cloth, Macmillan,* 1868—Denison (Sir Wm.) Varieties of Vice Regal Life, *map,* 2 vol. *cloth, Longmans,* 1870 (4)

158 Duffy (Sir Ch. G.) Four Years of Irish History, 1845-49, *Melbourne,* 1863—The League of North and South (Ireland), 1850-54, 1886—Letters and Extracts from the Writings of J. Beete Jukes, 1871 ; and others (6)

159 Dumont-D'Urville. Voyage autour du Monde, *numerous illustrations,* 2 vol. *half morocco imp. 8vo. Paris, Furne,* 1859

160 Dutton (Francis) South Australia and its Mines, with an historical Sketch of the Colony to the period of Capt. Grey's Departure, *map and plates, calf extra, m. e. by Rivière* Boone, 1846

161 Dutton (Fr.) South Australia and its Mines, *map and plates, Boone,* 1846—Kolff (D. H.) Voyages of the Dutch Brig of War Dourga to New Guinea, translated by G. W. Earl, *map,* 1840—West (Rev. T.) Ten Years of South-Central Polynesia, *portrait and maps,* 1865 ; and others (5)

162 Drury (Robert) Pleasant and Surprising Adventures during fifteen years' Captivity on the Island of Madagascar, *map and plates, old calf* W. Meadows, 1743

163 Drury. Madagascar, or Robert Drury's Journal during fifteen years' Captivity on that Island, *map and plates, half calf,* 1729

164 Earl (G. W.) Enterprise in Tropical Australia, *map,* 1846—Hursthouse (Ch.) Settlement of New Plymouth, N.Z. 1849—Campbell (Wm.) Crown Lands of Australia, 1855—Account of the Island of Mauritius, 1842 ; and others (9)

165 Earl (G. W.) Papuans (Norris's Ethnographical Library), *coloured plates, cloth,* 1853—Gilbert (Rev. T.) New Zealand Settlers and Soldiers, 1861—[Campbell (J. Logan)] Poenamo, Sketches of the Early Days of New Zealand, 1881—Australia as it is, by a Clergyman, 1867 ; and others (6)

166 Earle (Aug.) Narrative of a Nine Months' Residence in New Zealand in 1827, *map and plates, tree-calf extra, m. e. by Rivière* Longmans, 1832

167 Earle (Aug.) Narrative of a Nine Months' Residence in New Zealand in 1827, *plates, half morocco,* 1832—Tuckey (J. H.) Account of a Voyage to establish a Colony at Port Phillip, 1802-4, *half morocco,* 1805 (2)

168 Earle (H.) Ups and Downs, or Incidents of Australian Life, 1861 —Campbell-Praed (Mrs.) Australian Life, Black and White, *illustrated,* 1885— Rise and Progress of Australia, Tasmania and New Zealand, by an Englishman, 1857 ; &c. (5)

169 Early Voyages to Terra Australis, now called Australia, edited with Introduction by R. H. Major (with Appendix), *maps, half morocco* Hakluyt Society, 1859

170 Early Voyages to Terra Australis. Another Copy, *cloth, ib.* 1859

171 Earp (G. B.) The Gold Colonies of Australia, and Gold Seeker's Manual, *map,* 1852—Capper (John) Emigrant's Guide to Australia, 1853—Busby (Jas.) Culture of the Vine in New South Wales, 1840—History of Bullanabee and Clinkataboo, two recently discovered Islands in the Pacific, 1828—Port Phillip in 1849, by Dr. Clutterbuck, *map,* 1850 ; &c (12)

172 Eldershaw (F.) Australia as it really is, *coloured plates,* 1854— Handbook for New Zealand, *Parker,* 1848—British Colonization of New Zealand, *ib.* 1837—The New Zealanders, *L.E.K.* 1830 ; and others (9)

173 Ellis (Rev. W.) Polynesian Researches, during a Residence of Six Years in the South Sea Islands, *map and plate,* 2 vol. *half bound* Fisher, 1829

174 Emigrant Family ; the Story of an Australian Settler, 3 vol. *cloth,* 1849—Boldrewood (Ralph) Robbery under arms, 3 vol. 1888 —Reminiscences of a Veteran, *frontispieces,* 3 vol. 1861 (9)

175 Evans (G. W.) History and Description of Van Diemen's Land, *frontispiece* 1824

176 Evans. A Year in Tasmania, *map, Hobart Town, W. Fletcher,* 1854 —Evans (G. W.) History and Description of the Present State of Van Diemen's Land, *front. half morocco, J. Souter,* 1824 (2)

177 Eyre's (E. J.) Central Australia. Expeditions of Discovery, 2 vol. 1845

178 Fairfax (Wm.) Handbook to Australasia, *map, Melbourne,* 1859— Western Australia for the Use of Settlers, *map,* 1842—The Emigrant's Manual (Australia, New Zealand, America and South Africa), with Preface by J. Hill Burton, *Edinb.* 1851— Visit to the Antipodes by a Squatter, 1846 ; and others (8)

179 Farjeon (B. L.) Griff and the Golden Land, Doctor Middleton's Daughter, and a Desperate Character, 6 vol. ; and others (9)

180 Farmer (Sarah S.) Tonga and the Friendly Islands, *plates*, 1855— Bonwick (Jas.) First Twenty Years in Australia, 1882—Eden (Ch. H.) The Fifth Continent, with the Adjacent Islands, *S.P.C.K. ;* and others (6)

181 Favenc (Ernest) History of Australian Exploration from 1788 to 1888, *maps, plates and facsimiles, cloth imp. 8vo. Sydney,* 1888

182 Fenton (Jas.) History of Tasmania, 1642-1884, *map and coloured portraits, cloth, Tasmania, etc.* 1884—Smythe (Mrs.) Ten Months in the Fiji Islands, *chromos and woodcuts,* 1864—Guillemard (A. G.) Over Land and Sea, 1875 (3)

183 Field (Barron) Geographical Memoirs of New South Wales, by Various Hands, *map and frontispiece, half calf J. Murray,* 1825

   ** The Appendix contains Field's " First Fruits of Australian Poetry," first privately printed in New South Wales in 1819, and Reviewed by Charles Lamb in the "Examiner," Jan. 16, 1820.

184 Field. Geographical Memoirs of New South Wales. Another copy, *frontispiece and maps, tree-calf extra, m. e. by Rivière*
                                                  ib. 1825

185 Financial Statements of the Colonial Treasurers of New South Wales, 1855-1881, with an Appendix by the Editor, Jas. Thomson, *photos, morocco roy. 8vo. Sydney, T. Richards,* 1881

186 Flanagan (R.) History of New South Wales, 2 vol. *cloth*
                                            Sampson Low, 1862

187 Fornander (Abraham) Account of the Polynesian Race, 3 vol. *cloth*   *Trübner,* 1878

188 Forrest (John) Explorations in Australia, *portrait and illustrations by G. F. Angas, cloth, S. Low,* 1875—Forster (Anthony) South Australia, its Progress and Prosperity, *map,* 1866—Anderson (J. W.) Notes of Travel in Fiji and New Caledonia, *map and coloured plates*

189 Forrest (John) Explorations in Australia, *maps and illustrations by G. F. Angas, cloth,* 1875—Woods (Rev. J. E.) Geological Observations in South Australia, *illustrated, cloth,* 1862 (2)

190 Foster (J. F. L.) New Colony of Victoria, formerly Port Philip, 1851—Money (Ch. L.) Knocking about in New Zealand, *Melbourne,* 1871—Caird (J. A. H.) Notes on Sheep Farming in New Zealand, *plates,* 1874 ; and others (11)

191 Fox (Lady Mary) Account of an Expedition into the interior of New Holland, 1837—Ward (Jas.) A History of Gold, *W. S. Orr, n. d.*—Mossman (S.) Gold Regions of Australia, *ib.*— Mackenzie (Rev. D.) The Gold Digger, *ib.*—Curr (E.) Van Diemen's Land, 1824—Mitchell (Sir T. L.) Australian Geography, *Sydney,* 1850 ; and others ; *all half bound* (6)

16

192   Franklin (Sir John). Narrative of some Passages in the History of Van Diemen's Land, during the last three Years of Sir John Franklin's Administration of its Government, *calf gilt, by Rivière, not published*, 1845

193   Franklin. Home Passages in the History of Van Diemen's Land during the last Three Years of Sir John Franklin's Government *(top of title cut), not published*   n. d.

194   Frere (Alice M.) The Antipodes and Round the World, Australia, New Zealand, etc. *numerous illustrations, cloth, Hatchards*, 1870 —Byrne (J. C.) Twelve Years Wanderings in the British Colonies, 1835-47, *maps*, 2 vol. *cloth, R. Bentley*, 1848   (3)

195   [Gardiner (Capt. Allen)] The Friend of Australia, a Plan for exploring the Interior, by a Retired Officer, *map and coloured plates, half calf*, 1830—Kolff (D. H.) Voyages of the Dutch Brig Dourga through the Moluccan Archipelago, translated by G. W. Earl, *maps, half calf*, 1840   (2)

196   Geographical Society of Australasia (Proceedings) vol. I-IV and special vol. *Sydney, T. Richards*, 1885-8—Journal of the Royal Geographical Society, vol. I and XLIX, Supplementary Papers, vol. I, Pt. 1 ; etc.   (10)

197   Giles (Ernest) Australia twice traversed ; Narrative of Five Exploring Expeditions through Australia 1872-76, *numerous illustrations*, 2 vol. *cloth (presentation copy) Sampson Low*, 1889

198   Gill (S. T.) The Diggers and Diggings of Australia, 30 *lithograph scenes, bound in a vol. oblong, Melbourne*, 1855—The Australian Temperance Magazine, vol. I, *Sydney*, 1838—Godwin's Emigrant's Guide to Van Diemen's Land, *map and view*, 1823—Documents laid before Lord Glenelg, by Sir G. S. Mackenzie relative to the Convicts sent to New South Wales, April 1836; *all half bound*   (4)

199   Gisborne (Wm.) New Zealand Rulers and Statesmen, 1840-85, *portraits*, 1886—Otter (R. H.) Winters Abroad, 1882—Phillips (J. A.) Gold-Mining and Assaying, 1852—Clarke (Rev. W. B.) Researches in the Southern Gold Fields, *Sydney*, 1860 ; &c. (6)

200   Godwin. Emigrant's Guide to Van Diemen's Land, *map and folding frontispiece*, 1823—Cruise (R. A.) Ten Months Residence in New England, *frontispiece*, 1823—Memoir of R. B. Vaughan, Archbp. of Sydney, by J. C. Hedley, 1884 ; *all half bound*   (3)

201   Gold Fields of Victoria (The) in 1862, *Melbourne*, 1863—Aspinall (Clara) Three Years in Melbourne, *L. Booth*, 1862—Allen (C. H.) Visit to Queensland and her Goldfields, 1870—Alfred Dudley, or the Australian Settlers, *plates*, 1830 ; and others (6)

202   Goodridge (Ch. Medyett) Narrative of a Voyage to the South Seas and the Shipwreck of the Princess of Wales Cutter, *plates*, 1847—St. Julian and Silvester, Productions, Industry and Resources of New South Wales, *Sydney*, 1853—British Colonization of New Zealand, 1837—Blacklock (A.) Treatise on Sheep in Australia, 1848—Tales about America and Australia, by Peter Parley, *n. d.*   (5)

203 Gorst (J. E.) The Maori King, 1864—Townsend (J. P.) Rambles and Observations in New South Wales, 1849—Journal of a Deputation from the Wesleyan Conference to Australia and Polynesia, by the Rev. R. Young, 1854 ; and others (7)

204 Gorst (J. E.) The Maori King, or the Story of Our Quarrel with the Natives of New Zealand, 1864—Wildey (W. B.) Australasia and the Oceanic Region, *Melbourne,* 1876—Hill, What we saw in Australia, 1875—Lundie (G. A.) Missionary Life in Samoa, 1846 ; and others (6)

205 Gould (John) Introduction to the Birds of Australia, *cloth, printed for the author,* 1848—Buller (W. L.) Classified List of Mr. S. Wm. Silver's Collection of New Zealand Birds, *woodcuts, white boards, imp. 8vo, Petherick,* 1888 (2)

206 Gould (John) Handbook to the Birds of Australia, 2 vol. *green cloth gilt* *roy. 8vo. Published by the author,* 1865

207 Grad (A. Ch.) L'Australe Intérieure, Explorations 1860-62, *half morocco* *Paris,* 1864

208 Grammar and Vocabulary of the Language of New Zealand, published by the Church Missionary Society, *half morocco* *Seeley,* 1820

209 Grant (Jas.) Verhaal van eene Ondekkingsreise na Nieuw-Zuid-Wales, *Haarlem,* 1805—Henniker (Sir F.) Reis naar Egypte, etc. *plates, Dordrecht,* 1825—Oxley (John) Reizen in de Binnenlanden van Australie, *ib.* 1821 ; and others (8)

210 Greene (W. T.) Birds I have kept, *coloured plates,* 1885—Dulcken (H. W.) The World's Explorers, *n. d.*—The New British Province of South Australia, *Knight,* 1835 ; and others (7)

211 Greene (W. T.) Parrots in Captivity, 3 vol. *coloured plates, cloth imp. 8vo. Bell,* 1884-7

212 Grey (George) Journals of Two Expeditions of Discovery in North-West and Western Australia, 1837-39, 2 vol. *maps and illustrations, tree calf extra, m. e. by Riviere* *Boone,* 1841

213 Grey (Geo.) Another copy, 2 vol. *maps and plates, cloth ib.* 1841

QUARTO.

214 Astrolabe (Voyage de Découvertes de l') 1826-29, Observations Nautiques, Météorologiques, Hydrographiques et de Physique, *cloth* *Paris,* 1833

215 Australia. A Collection of 30 Plates of Views, Natural History, Aborigines, etc. by W. V. Blandowski, *in a portfolio*

216 Australia, by E. C. Booth, 2 vol. *illustrated with fine steel engravings from drawings by Skinner Prout, N. Chevalier, etc. half morocco* *Virtue & Co.*

217 Australian Aboriginals Photographed, by J. W. Lindt, *Grafton 8 photos. loose in cloth portfolio*

C

218 Australian Ladies' Annual, *first year of publication, Melbourne,* 1878 —Patchett Martin, Fernshawe, *ib.* 1882—Geological Survey of Victoria, Report of Progress, by R. B. Smith, *ib. n. d.*— Railway Guide of New South Wales, FIRST EDITION, *Sydney,* 1881 ; and others (6)

219 Australian Picture Pleasure Book, 200 *illustrations, cloth*
Sydney, J. R. Clarke, 1857

220 Australian Portrait Gallery and Memoirs of Representative Colonial Men, etc. *portraits, morocco gilt*
Sydney, Southern Cross Pub. Co. n. d.

221 Blair (David) History of Australasia, from the First Dawn of Discovery to the Establishment of Free Government, *maps and numerous illustrations, morocco* *Glasgow, etc.* 1878

222 Blair (D.) Cyclopædia of Australasia, or Dictionary of Facts, etc. from the Earliest Dawn of Discovery in the Southern Ocean, to 1881, *cloth* *Melbourne, Fergusson,* 1881

223 Bligh (Wm.) Narrative of the Mutiny of the Bounty, *plan of ship and charts, half morocco (Large Copy)* *G. Nicol,* 1790

224 Bligh (Lieut. Wm.) Voyage to the South Sea in H.M.S. The Bounty, with an Account of the Mutiny on board the same ship, etc. *portrait, charts and plates, calf* *G. Nicol,* 1792

225 Bligh. Voyage to the South Sea, etc. Another copy, *portrait, charts, etc. calf* 1792

226 Brees (S. C.) Pictorial Illustrations of New Zealand, 67 *views and map, cloth* *John Williams,* 1847

227 Brees. New Zealand, Another Copy *(no map, plates foxed), cloth* 1847

228 Brown (Rob.) General Remarks, Geographical and Systematical on the Botany of Terra Australis, *half morocco W. Bulmer,* 1814

229 Brown (R.) Prodromus Floræ Novae-Hollandiae et Insulae Van-Diemen, *half morocco* *Veneunt a Redactione Isidis, Lips.* 1821

230 BULLER (W. L.) HISTORY OF THE BIRDS OF NEW ZEALAND, 35 *beautiful coloured plates, half morocco gilt, t. e. g.*
Van Voorst, 1873

231 Buller. BIRDS OF NEW ZEALAND, SECOND EDITION, 2 vol. 48 *beautiful coloured plates and woodcuts, whole red morocco gilt, g. e.* 1888

232 Burney (Jas.) Chronological History of the Discoveries in the South Sea or Pacific Ocean, 5 vol. in 4, *maps, calf* 1803-17

233 Cassell's Picturesque Europe. The British Isles, vol. I, *numerous illustrations, cloth gilt*

234 COLLINS (DAVID) ACCOUNT OF THE ENGLISH COLONY IN NEW SOUTH WALES, with some particulars of New Zealand, *maps and plates, half calf* *Cadell,* 1798

235 Collins (David) Account of the English Colony of New South Wales, with some particulars of New Zealand, &c. 2 vol. *maps and plates, calf (rebacked)* *ib.* 1798-1802

236 Coloured Views of Van Diemen's Land, by J. Lycett (6)—Coloured View of Sydney (7)

237   COOK (CAPT.) THREE VOYAGES ROUND THE WORLD, 8 vol. *numerous maps and plates, and folio atlas, whole russia gilt, with arms on backs* (STOURHEAD COPY)   ·   1773-84

238   Cook. Three Voyages, with Forster's Account of the Second Voyage, and Kippis's Life of Cook, 11 vol. *4to and folio atlas, uniform half calf gilt*   1773-88

239   Cook. First Voyage, by Hawkesworth, 2 vol. and folio Atlas of Maps and Plates   1773, *etc.*

240   Cook. Journal of a Voyage Round the World in H.M.S. Endeavour, 1768-71, with a Concise Vocabulary of the Language of Otaheite, *half morocco*   *T. Becket*, 1771

241   Cook. Journal of a Voyage Round the World in H.M.S. Endeavour, 1768-71, another copy, *half bound*   *ib.* 1771

242   Coveny (Christopher) Twenty Scenes from the Works of Dickens, designed and etched by Christ. Coveney, *fine proof impressions, half morocco*   *Sydney, T. H. Fielding*, 1882

243   Dalrymple (Alex.) Historical Collection of the Several Voyages and Discoveries in the South Pacific Ocean, *maps and plates, calf, J. Nourse*, 1769—Letter from Mr. Dalrymple to Dr. Hawkesworth occasioned by some groundless and illiberal Imputations in his Account of the Late Voyages to the South, *half bound, scarce, ib.* 1773   (2)

244   Dalrymple (Alex.) Historical Collection of the Several Voyages and Discoveries in the South Pacific Ocean, 2 vol. in 1, *maps and plates, half morocco*   *J. Nourse*, 1770

245   David (T. W. Edgeworth) Geology of the Vegetable Creek Tin-Mining Field, New England District, New South Wales, *maps and sections, half morocco*   *Sydney, C. Potter*, 1887

246   Dawson (Jas.) Australian Aborigines, the Languages and Customs of several Tribes of Aborigines in the Western District of Victoria, Australia, *photos. and facsimile, cloth*   *Melbourne, G. Robertson*, 1881

247   Delessert (Eug.) Voyages dans les deux Océans Atlantique et Pacifique, *numerous illustrations, half morocco*   *sup. imp. 8vo. Paris, A. Franck*, 1848

248   Demon McGuire (The) [in Verse], *curious satirical prints, Sydney, Gibbs, Shallard & Co. n. d.*—Southerly Busters, by Ironbark (H. Gibson), *profusely illustrated by Alf. Clint, Sydney*, 1878—Coutts (J.) Vacation Tours, *illustrated, Melbourne*, 1880—In Southern Seas, a Trip to the Antipodes, by "Petrel," *illustrated, Edin.* 1888   (4)

249   Discoveries of the French in 1768 and 1769, to the South-east of New Guinea, with Abridgment of the Voyages and Discoveries of the Spaniards in the same Seas, translated from the French, *maps, half morocco*   *Stockdale*, 1791

250   Duncan's Weekly Register of Politics, Facts and General Literature, 2 vol. *all published*, Editor W. A. Duncan, *Sydney*, 1843-4

251   Elouis (E.) Tables for Standarding Gold, according to Assay Reports decimally Expressed, *half bound*   *Sydney, T. Richards*, 1872

252 Eredia (Godinho de) Malaca, L'Inde Méridionale, et le Cathay, MS. original Autographe, reproduit en facsimile et traduit par Léon Janssen, *facsimile charts, etc. (only* 120 *copies printed), calf*
Bruxelles, C. Muquardt, 1882

253 Finn (Ed.) Chronicles of Early Melbourne, 1835-52, historical, personal and anecdotal, by Garryowen, 2 vol. *portraits and illustrations, brown morocco gilt, g. e. Melbourne, Fergusson,* 1888

254 FLINDERS (MATTHEW) VOYAGE TO TERRA AUSTRALIS, in 1801-1803, in H. M. S. Investigator, with Account of the Shipwreck of the Porpoise, etc. LARGE PAPER, 2 vol. *roy. 4to of text (with views), and elephant folio atlas of maps, etc. (text in russia, g. e. atlas, half bound)* *Bulmer,* 1814

255 Forrest (Capt. Thos.) Voyage to New Guinea and the Moluccas performed in the " Tartar" Galley, 1774-76, with a Vocabulary of the Magindano Tongue, *portrait, maps and plates, old calf (large copy)* *J. Robson, etc.* 1779

256 Forrest (Capt. Thos.) Another (smaller) copy, *calf, cracked* 1779

257 Fossil Organic Remains of Mammalia and Aves, in the Museum of the Royal College of Surgeons (Australia from p. 291), *cloth* *R. Taylor,* 1845

FOLIO.

258 Allen (F. H.) The Great Cathedrals of the World, 2 vol. 130 *plates in photogravure, half morocco, Boston, Haskell & Post, n. d.*

259 ANGAS (G. FRENCH) THE KAFIRS ILLUSTRATED, *portrait,* 30 *coloured plates, and woodcuts, half morocco*
imp. fol. Hogarth, n. d.

260 ANGAS. THE NEW ZEALANDERS ILLUSTRATED, *coloured title and* 60 *coloured plates, half red morocco gilt*
imp. fol. McLean, 1847

261 ANGAS. SOUTH AUSTRALIA ILLUSTRATED, 60 *coloured plates and coloured title, half morocco* *imp. fol. ib.* 1847

262 Angas. Views of the Gold Regions of Australia, 2 *lithograph titles and* 6 *plates, half morocco* *J. Hogarth,* 1851

263 Angas. Another copy, *original wrapper* 1851

264 Atlas (The) Sydney Weekly Journal of Politics, Commerce and Literature, vol. I-IV, Nov. 30, 1844, to Dec. 30, 1848, 4 vol. Editor Robert Lowe, Lord Sherbrooke, *half bound* *Sydney*
** This set has the initials of the writers appended to the leading articles.

265 Atlas of the Settled Counties of New South Wales, 20 *maps, half bound* *Sydney, Basch & Co. n. d.*

266 Australia (Facsimiles of Old Charts of) now in the British Museum, 4 *charts on* 8 *plates, loose in elephant portfolio*
Trübner, 1885

267 Australian Scenery. Forty-five fine large Photographs of Scenery and Buildings; and Two Photos. of Sir Francis Forbes, Chief Justice of N.S.W. *in an atlas folio scrap-book*

268 Australian Scenery. Two fine coloured Views, of Port Arthur
and Brady's Look-out on the Great Lake, Tasmania (2)

269 Australian Sketcher. With Pen and Pencil, No. II, May 17,
1873, to No. CXL, Dec. 31, 1881, in 2 vol. *half bound*
Melbourne

270 Australian Grasses. A Collection of Ninety-two Dried Specimens of, with MS. descriptions, mounted in a vol. *half bound*

271 Australian Irrigation Colonies on the River Murray in Victoria
and South Australia, *map and numerous illustrations, half
morocco* *imp. fol. Lond. Chaffey Bros. n. d.*

272 Australian Witness and Presbyterian Herald, Nos. 1-200, Nov. 2,
1872, to Aug. 26, 1876, in 2 vol. *half bound*—The Witness
and Australian Presbyterian, Nos. 1-135, Jan. 17, 1874, to
Aug. 12, 1876, *half bound*—The Testimony, Nos. I-LII, *cloth*,
Sydney, 1865-70—My Note Book, vol. IV, *Melbourne*, 1858—
The Farm and Garden, edited by E. W. Andrews, *Adelaide*,
1859 (6)

273 AUSTRALIAN PARLIAMENT (ACTS OF). Statutes of New South
Wales, Public and Private, from 1879 to 1887, *Sydney*—The
Statute Index, 1824-74, by A. Oliver, *half bound, ib.* 1874 (12)

274 AUSTRALIAN PARLIAMENTARY REPORTS. Gold Mines and Geology of Victoria, 1853-75, in 3 vol. *numerous maps and plates,
cloth*

275 Australian Parliamentary Reports. Papers relative to the Recent
Discovery of Gold in Australia, 2 vol. *maps and plates, cloth*
1852-3

276 Australian Parliamentary Reports. Reports on the Gold, Coal
and Tin Fields of New South Wales, 2 vol. *maps and plates,
cloth* 1857-82

277 Australian Parliamentary Reports. Reports of the Mining Surveyors and Registrars of Victoria, 3 vol. *maps and plates, cloth*
1864-6-7

278 Australian Parliamentary Reports. Burke and Wills. Australian
Exploring Expedition (several papers), *in* 1 *vol. maps* 1858-62

279 Australian Parliamentary Reports. The War in New Zealand
and Affairs of the Colony, 2 vol. *maps, etc. cloth* 1862-81, *etc.*

280 Australian Parliamentary Reports. Australian Industrial
Resources (thick vol.) *maps, cloth* 1857-66

281 Australian Parliamentary Reports. First Survey and Settlement
of Port Phillip, *map*, 1878—Progress and Final Reports of
the Exploration Committee of the Royal Society of Victoria,
1863—Journal of Expedition from De Grey River to Port
Darwin, by A. Forrest, *plates and map*, 1880—Exploration
Expedition (Commander Norman & Burke & Wills), 1861-2 (4)

282 Australian Parliamentary Reports. Navigation of the Murray
River — Oyster Fisheries — The Taranaki Question and
Seignorial Right—Forrest (A.) Journal of Expedition from
De Grey River to Port Darwin, *maps and plates*, 1880—Six
Maps of the Provinces of Auckland and Nelson, 1864; and 1
other (5)

283 Australian Parliamentary Reports. Reports on the Aborigines
    of Victoria, 1853, &c.—Select Committee on Aborigines
    British Settlements, 1837   (2)

284 Australian Parliamentary Reports. Melbourne Town Council
    Proceedings, 1847-50, 2 vol.   *Melbourne*

285 Australian Parliamentary Reports. Meteorological Observations
    at the Adelaide Observatory during 1882, by Ch. Todd,
    morocco, Adelaide, 1885—Report on Colonial Military Expen-
    diture, 1834—Report on School Buildings, New South Wales,
    1880 ; and others   (8)

286 Australian Parliamentary Reports. Census of New South Wales,
    1851-4—Waste Lands of New South Wales, 1843, &c.—Report
    on Shipwrecks, 1836   (3)

SECOND DAY'S SALE.

OCTAVO ET INFRA.

Lot 287.

REY (Capt. G.) Vocabulary of the Dialects of Western Australia, 1841—Bunce (D.) Language of the Aborigines of Victoria, *Geelong*, 1859—Kamilaroi Sayings, by Wm. Ridley, *woodcuts, Sydney*, 1856 ; and 1 other (4)

288 Grey (Capt. G.) Vocabulary of the Dialects of South Western Australia, *half bound, Boone*, 1840—Ridley (Wm.) Kamilaroi Sayings, *woodcuts, Sydney*, 1856 (2)

289 Grey (Sir Geo.) Polynesian Mythology, and Ancient Traditional History of the New Zealand Race, *plates (Author's signature on title), mottled morocco* J. Murray, 1855

290 Grey (Sir Geo.) Polynesian Mythology, Another copy, *green cloth* ib. 1855

291 Gudgeon (T. W.) Reminiscences of the War in New Zealand, *portraits*, 1879—Peck (B. C.) Recollections of Sydney, 1850—Annals of the Diocese of New Zealand, 1856—Shipwreck of the Admella, *Melbourne*, 1859 ; and others (12)

292 Haast (Jul. von) Geology of the Provinces of Canterbury and Westland, *N. Z. plates, Christchurch*, 1879—Macartney (J. N.) The Bendigo Goldfield Registry, *plans, Melbourne*, 1872—Bird (S. D.) On Australian Climates and Pulmonary Consumption, 1863 ; and others (7)

293 Hannaford (Sam.) Jottings in Australia, *Melbourne*, 1856—Handbook for New Zealand, *Parker*, 1848—Eden (Ch. H.) My Wife and I in Queensland, 1872—Saunders (Th.) Settlement of Port Flinders and the Province of Albert, 1853—Curr (E.) Three Years in Van Diemen's Land, 1834—Mackenzie (Rev. D.) Emigrant's Guide to Australia, 1845 (6)

294 Hannaford (S.) Jottings in Australia, *Melbourne*, 1856—The Victorian Miner's Manual, *ib. n. d.*—The Four Colonies of Australia, *Cradock & Co.*—Hull (H. M.) Forty Years in Tasmania, 1859—Ireland (A.) Geography and History of Oceania, *map, Tasmania*, 1861 ; and others (7)

295 Harcus (Wm.) South Australia, its History, Resources and Productions, *maps and illustrations, cloth, S. Low*, 1876—Buller (Rev. Jas.) Forty Years in New Zealand, *portrait and illustrations, cloth, Hodder*, 1878 (2)

296 Harvie-Linklater (Fred.) Statutes relating to Equity and Lunacy in force in New South Wales, *half calf*
imp. 8vo. Sydney, T. Richards, 1879

297 Haswell (W. A.) Catalogue of the Australian Stalk and Sessile-Eyed Crustacea, *plates, Sydney,* 1882—Graham (J. R.) Treatise on the Australian Merino, *Melbourne,* 1870—Southey (Thos.) Colonial Sheep and Wool, 1851—Wilson (Sam.) Angora Goat, *Melbourne,* 1873—Mitchell (Graham) Cumberland Disease in Australian Sheep, *ib.* 1877—Bruce (Alex.) Report on Pleuro-Pneumonia in New South Wales, *Sydney,* 1868—Ramsay (E. P.) Catalogue of Australian Birds in the Australian Museum, part III (Psittaci), *ib.* 1891 ; and others   (12)

298 Hay (W. Delisle) Brighter Britain ! or Settler and Maori in Northern New Zealand, 2 vol. *cloth*   *R. Bentley,* 1882

299 Haydon (G. H.) Five Years Experience of Australia Felix, with Short Account of its early settlement and its present position, *illustrations on stone by H. Hainsselin, tree-calf gilt, m. e. by Rivière*   *imp. 8vo. Hamilton Adams,* 1846

299* Haydon (G. H.) The Australian Emigrant, *illustrated by Watts Phillips, Hull*   *Virtue & Co.* 1854

300 Haydon (G. H.) The Golden Colony ; or, Victoria in 1854, *map and illustrations*   1855

301 Hazlewood (Rev. D.) A Feejeean and English Dictionary and Grammar *(imperfect), Vewa Feejee,* 1850—Bible in Malagese, *Lond.* 1851—Joshua to Esther in Samoese, *Samoa,* 1854—Testament in Fiji, *Lond.* 1870 ; and others   (5)

302 Hearn (W. E.) The Aryan Household, its Structure and Development, *cloth, Melbourne, G. Robertson,* 1878 — Broughton (Bp. W. G. of Sidney) Sermons on the Church of England, 1857—Low (H.) Sarawak, its Inhabitants and Productions, *plates, cloth,* 1848—The Missionary Guide Book, *woodcuts,* 1846   (4)

303 Heaton (J. H.) Australian Dictionary of Dates and Men of the Time, 1542-1879, *crimson morocco, g. e. by Mansell*
imp. 8vo. Sydney, G. Robertson, 1879

304 Heaton (J. H.) Australian Dictionary, eight copies, *cloth*   *ib.*

305 Henderson (John) Observations on the Colonies of New South Wales, and Van Diemen's Land, *plates, tree-calf extra by Rivière*
Calcutta, Baptist Mission Press, 1832

306 Henderson (John) Observations on the Colonies of New South Wales and Van Diemen's Land, 2 *plates, half morocco*
Calcutta, 1832

307 Henderson (John) Excursions and Adventures in New South Wales, 2 vol. in 1, *map and plates, cloth,* 1851—Griffiths (Ch.) Present State and Prospects of the Port Phillip District of New South Wales, *frontispiece, Dubl.* 1845—Earl (G. Windsor) Enterprise in Tropical Australia, *map,* 1846 ; and others (6)

308 Henderson (John) Excursions and Adventures in New South Wales, 2 vol. *frontispieces, half bound,* 1851—The New Zealanders, *C. Knight,* 1830—Fitton (E. B.) New Zealand, *map,* 1856 —Settlers and Convicts, 1847—Earp (G. Butler) Gold Colonies of Australia, 1852—Fox (Wm.) The Six Colonies of New Zealand, 1851 ; and others   (12)

309 Henniker (Sir Fr.) Notes of a Visit to Egypt, Nubia, the Oasis Boeris, Mount Sinai and Jerusalem, *second edition, tree-calf extra, by Cecil and Larkins* *J. Murray*, 1824

310 Hill (Rosamond and Florence) What we saw in Australia, *half bound*, 1875—Bartlett (Thos.) New Holland, its Colonization, Productions and Resources, 1843—Stretton (Chas.) Memoirs of a Chequered Life (Victoria during the Digging Fever, etc.) 3 vol. *portrait*, 1862 ; and another (6)

311 History of New South Wales, compiled from the best and most recent Authorities, by a Literary Gentleman, *map and plates, half bound* *Newcastle-upon-Tyne*, 1811

312 History of New South Wales by O'Hara, *half calf*, 1817—Parker (Capt. J.) Voyage round the World in the 'Gorgon,' 1795— Narrative of the Sufferings of T. F. Palmer and W. Skirving during a Voyage to New South Wales, on board the Surprise Transport, *Camb.* 1797—Description of Corsica, by Frederick, son of King Theodore of Corsica, *map*, 1795, in 1 vol. *half bound* (2)

313 Historical MSS. Commission. Twelfth Report, Appendix, parts I-X (wanting part III) ; parts II, III and IV of the Hatfield MSS. and duplicates of parts I-II of the Cowper MSS. ; together 14 parts, *unbound* 1888-91

314 Hobart Town Directory and General Guide, *cloth, narrow imp. 8vo. Hobart Town, J. Moore, July*, 1852—Ross's Hobart Town Almanack and Van Diemen's Land Annual for 1835, *frontispiece, cloth, Hobart Town, J. Ross* (2)

315 Hodder (E.) Memoirs of New Zealand Life, 1862—What we did in Australia, edited by G. B. Earp, 1853—Kingston (W. H. G.) How to Emigrate, 1850 ; and others (10)

316 Hodgkinson (Clement) Australia from Port Macquarie to Moreton Bay, with descriptions of the Natives, their Manners and Customs, *map and plates, half calf gilt* *Boone*, 1845

317 Hodgkinson (Cl.) Australia from Port Macquarie to Moreton Bay, *map and plates, Boone*, 1845—Martin (S. M. D.) New Zealand, in a Series of Letters, 1845—Wells (W. H.) Gazetteer of the Australian Colonies, *plates, Sydney*, 1848—Jukes (J. Beete) Sketch of the Physical Structure of Australia, *Boone*, 1850 ; and others (6)

318 Hodgson (C. P.) Reminiscences of Australia with Hints on the Squatter's Life, 1846—Peck (G. W.) Melbourne and the Chincha Islands, *New York*, 1854—Russell (P.) Australian Tales and Sketches, *n. d.*—Stone (O. C.) A Few Months in New Guinea, *illustrated*, 1880 ; and others (7)

319 Hodgson (C. P.) Reminiscences of Australia, with Hints on the Squatter's Life, *frontispiece and map, calf gilt*, 1846—Cunningham (P.) Hints for Australian Emigrants, *calf gilt*, 1841— Balfour (J. O.) A Sketch of New South Wales, *calf gilt*, 1845 (3)

320 Holman (Jas.) Voyage round the World, including Travels in Africa, Asia, Australasia, America, etc. 1827-32, 4 vol. *portrait and plates, cloth* *Smith, Elder*, 1834

321 Holt (Joseph) Irish Rebel. Memoirs, edited from his Original MS. by T. C. Croker, 2 vol. *portrait and facsimiles, half morocco* *Colburn*, 1838

322 Hood (John) Australia and the East, a Journal Narrative of a Voyage to New South Wales, &c. *calf, J. Murray*, 1843— Roberts (Jane) Narrative of a Voyage to the Swan River and Van Diemen's Land, 1829-31, *frontispiece, calf*, 1834—Powell (Rev. J. G.) Narrative of a Voyage to the Swan River, etc. *map, calf*, 1831 (3)

323 Hovell (W. H.) and H. Hume. Journey of Discovery to Port Phillip in 1824-5, *map* *Sydney*, 1837

324 Howitt (Wm.) History of Discovery in Australia, Tasmania, and New Zealand, from the earliest date to present day, 2 vol. *maps, cloth* *Longmans*, 1865

325 Howitt (Wm.). Land Labour and Gold, or Two Years in Victoria, 2 vol. *cloth*, 1855—Colonization and Christianity, 1838—A Boy's Adventures in the Wilds of Australia, 1854 (4)

326 Howitt (Rich.) Impressions of Australia Felix, *frontispiece*, 1845 —Chamerovzon (L. A.) The New Zealand Question and the Rights of Aborigines, 1848—Hargraves (E. H.) Australia and its Gold Fields, *portrait and map*, 1855—Phillips (J. A.) Gold Mining and Assaying, *woodcuts*, 1852 ; and others (6)

327 Hübner (Baron) Through the British Empire, 2 vol. *map*, 1886 —Tucker (Rev. H. W.) Memoir of the Life and Episcopate of Bp. G. A. Selwyn, 2 vol. *portraits and maps*, 1879 (4)

328 Hughes (Wm.) The Australian Colonies ; their Origin and Present Condition, 1852— Smith (Sidney) The Settler's New Home, or the Emigrant's Location, 2 parts in 1 vol. 1849— Harris (Alex.) Martin Beck, the Story of an Australian Settler, 1852—Settlers and Convicts, by A. Harris, 1847 (4)

329 Hunter (John) Historical Journal of the Transactions at Port Jackson and Norfolk Island, including the Journals of Governors Phillip and King, *portrait, map and plates, margin of title shaved, half calf* 1792

330 Hursthouse (Ch.) Account of the Settlement of New Plymouth, New Zealand, *plan and views, tree-calf gilt, by Rivière*, 1849— Marjoribanks (Alex.) Travels in New South Wales and New Zealand, 2 vol. *calf gilt*, 1847-50 (3)

331 Hursthouse (Ch.) New Zealand, or Zealandia the Britain of the South, 2 vol. *tinted plates, cloth*, 1857—Lang (J. D.) Historical and Statistical Account of New South Wales, 2 vol. *cloth*, 1834—Kelly (Wm.) Life in Victoria, 2 vol. in 1, *half calf*, 1859 (5)

332 Illustrated Australian Magazine, 3 vol. in 1, *plates, with all faults as there is no title to vol. III, half bound* *Melbourne, Ham Brothers*, 1850-51

333 Irwin (Capt. F. Chidley) State and Position of Western Australia, commonly called the Swan River Settlement, *tree-calf gilt, m. e. by Rivière* *Simpkin & Co.* 1835

334 Irwin (Capt. F. Chidley) State and Position of Western Australia, commonly called the Swan River Settlement, 1835—Beecham (John) Colonization; with an Examination of the Proposals of the Association for the Colonization of New Zealand, 1838—Whately (Archbp.) Remarks on Transportation, 1834—Papers Read at the Church Congress, *Melbourne*, 1882; *all half bound* (4)

335 Jackson (Andrew) Robert O'Hara Burke and the Australian Exploring Expedition of 1860, *map*, 1862—Brodie (W.) Pitcairn's Island and the Islanders, 1851—Majoribanks (A.) Travels in New South Wales, 1847—Horn (R. H.) Australian Facts and Prospects, 1859; and others (11)

336 James (T. H.) Six Months in South Australia, *map*, 1838—Malone (R. E.) Three Years' Cruise in the Australian Colonies, 1854—Alfred Dudley, or the Australian Settlers, *plates*, *Harvey & Darton*, 1830; and others (8)

337 James (T. H.) Six Months in South Australia, with Advice to Emigrants, *map*, *Lond. J. Cross*, 1838—Clarke (Rev. W. B.) Researches in the Southern Gold Fields of New South Wales, *map (torn and stained), Sydney*, 1860—Capper (Henry) South Australia, *third edition, map* (1839)—Counsel for Emigrants, *map, Aberdeen*, 1838—Coles' Guide to Melbourne, 1880 (5)

338 Jameson (R. G.) New Zealand, South Australia, and New South Wales, *maps, tree-calf extra, m. e. by Rivière Smith Elder*, 1842

339 Jardine. Overland Expedition from Rockhampton to Cape York, Northern Queensland *Brisbane*, 1867

340 Jeffreys (Lieut. Chas.) Van Diemen's Land, Geographical and Descriptive Delineations of, *half bound*, 1820—Cruise (R. A.) Ten Months' Residence in New Zealand, 1823 (2)

341 Jessop (W. R. H.) Sketches in Australia, 2 vol. in 1, *frontispiece, n. d.*—Earle (H.) Ups and Downs, or Incidents in Australian Life, *n. d.*—Russell (P.) Australian Tales and Sketches, *n. d.*—Australia, the Land of Promise, 1854; and others (9)

342 Johnston. Court Martial on Lieut.-Col. G. Johnston for deposing Wm. Bligh from the Governorship of New South Wales, *half morocco, very rare* 1811

343 Journals and Reports of Two Voyages to the Glenelg River, and the North-West Coast of Australia, 1863-4, *map, Perth (W. A.)*, 1864—Rusden (G. W.) Notes on New Zealand (" Priviledged and Confidential "), *autograph letter inserted* (1885)—Macdonald (Rev. D.) Oceania Linguistic and Anthropological, *Melbourne*, 1889—Australian Handbooks issued by the Emigrants' Information Office (6), 1887; and other pamphlets *a parcel*

344 Journals of Several Expeditions made in Western Australia, 1829-32, *map*, 1833—Hannaford (S.) Wild Flowers of Tasmania, *plates, Melbourne*, 1866—Lee (Mrs. R.) Adventures in Australia, *illustrated*, 1853—The New Zealanders, *C. Knight*, 1830; and others (8)

345 Journals of Several Expeditions made in Western Australia, 1829-32, *maps, J. Cross*, 1833—Parker (H. W.) Rise, Progress and Present State of Van Diemen's Land, 1833—Curr (E.) Van Diemen's Land, 1824—Earp (G. B.) Gold Colonies of Australia, 1852; and others (15)

346 Journal of an Expedition Overland from Auckland to Taranaki, undertaken in the Summer of 1849-50 by his Excellency (Sir George Grey) the Governor-in-Chief of New Zealand (in English and Maori), *cloth, very scarce*
Auckland, Williamson & Wilson, 1851

347 Journal of Australasia, 2 vol. *(illustrations in vol. II), half bound (not uniform) Melbourne, G. Slater*, 1856-57

348 Journal of Australasia. Another copy *ib.*

349 Jukes (J. Beete) Narrative of the Surveying Voyage of H.M.S. Fly in Torres Strait, New Guinea, &c. during 1842-46, 2 vol. *maps and plates, calf gilt, m. e. by Rivière Boone*, 1847

350 Jung (Dr. K. E.) Der Welttheil Australien, *numerous illustrations*, 4 vol. *Prag.* 1882—La Billardière, Reise nach dem Südmeer, *plates, Hamb.* 1801—Meinicke (C. G.) Das Festland Australien, 2 vol. *Prenzlau*, 1837—Flinders (M.) Reise nach dem Austral Lande aus dem Englischen von J. Götze, 2 vol. *Wiemar*, 1816; and others (11)

351 Kelly (A. C.) The Vine in Australia, *Melbourne*, 1862—Sutton (Geo.) Culture of the Grape-Vine and Orange in Australia and New Zealand, 1843—Fuller (Fr.) Five Years Residence in New Zealand, 1859—Burton (J. H.) The Emigrant's Manual, *Edinb.* 1851; and others (6)

352 Kelly (Wm.) Life in Victoria in 1853 and 1858, 2 vol. *cloth, Chapman and Hall*, 1859—Jessop (W. R. H.) Flindersland and Sturtland, or the Inside and Outside of Australia, 2 vol. *cloth, R. Bentley*, 1862 (4)

353 Kennaway (L. J.) Crusts; a Settler's Fare due South, *plates*, 1874—Silver's Handbook to South Africa, 1891—Louis (A.) An Exile's Romance, *New York*, 1887—Russell (Bp. M.) Polynesia, 1850; and others (9)

354 King (Capt. Ph. P.) Narrative of a Survey of the intertropical and Western Coasts of Australia, 1818-22, 2 vol. *plates charts and woodcuts, half calf J. Murray*, 1827

355 King (Capt. Ph. P.) Another copy, 2 vol. *boards, uncut ib.* 1827

356 Kittle (S.) Concise History of the Colony and Natives of New South Wales, *plates, half bound*
Edinb. Oliver & Boyd, n. d. (1814)

357 Kittle (S.) Concise History of the Colony and Natives of New South Wales, *plates Edinb. n. d.*

358 Labilliere (J. P.) Early History of the Colony of Victoria, 2 vol. *cloth, Sampson Low*, 1878—Williams (Bp. W.) Christianity among the New Zealanders, *illustrated*, 1867—Jobson (Dr. F. J.) Australia, &c. *coloured frontispiece*, 1862— Hogan (J. F.) The Australian in London, 1880 (5)

359 Lancelot (F.) Australia as it is ; its Settlements, Farms and Gold Fields, 2 vol. *frontispiece and plan, calf gilt, m. e. by Riviere* *Colburn*, 1852

360 Landor (E. W.) The Bushman ; or, Life in a New Country, *plates, tree-calf gilt, R. Bentley*, 1847—Forbes (Litton) Two Years in Fiji, *half calf, Longmans*, 1875—Hannah (Rev. S. W.) Notes of a Visit to Some Parts of Haïti, 1835, *calf gilt, Seeley*, 1836 (3)

361 Lang (J. D.) Phillipsland ; or, the Country hitherto designated Port Phillip, *map, Edinb.* 1847—Parkes (Sir Henry) Australian Views of England, 1869—Mossman and Banister. Australia Visited and Revisited, *map*, 1853 ; and others (5)

362 Lang (J. D.) Australian Emigrant's Manual, 1852—Dixon (Jas.) Narrative of a Voyage to New South Wales and Van Diemen's Land in the Ship Skelton in 1820, *frontispiece, Edinb.* 1822—Observations on the Colony of New South Wales for the Use of Mechanics and Labourers, 1836—Norris (Rev. W.) Annals of the Diocese of Adelaide, 1852—Buckton (T. J.) Western Australia, *map*, 1840 ; and 1 other (6)

363 Lang (J. D.) Australian Emigrant's Manual, 1852—Port Phillip in 1849, by J. B. Clutterbuck, *map*, 1850—Hussey (H.) The Australian Colonies (1855)—Leslie-Foster (J. F.) Port Phillip, 1851 ; and others (12)

364 Lang (J. D.) Historical and Statistical Account of New South Wales, 2 vol. *third edition, maps, half calf*, 1852—Cunningham (P.) Two Years in New South Wales, 2 vol. *second edition, maps, calf*, 1827 (4)

365 Lang (J. D.) Historical and Statistical Account of New South Wales, 2 vol. *fourth edition, map, cloth, Sampson Low*, 1875—De Beauvoir (Marq.) Voyage Round the World (Australia, Java, Siam, Canton), 2 vol. *cloth, Murray*, 1870 (4)

366 Lang (J. D.) Neu-Südwales, aus dem Englischen, *half bound, Quedlinburg*, 1840 — Chalmers and Gill, Neuguinea, autorisirte deutsche Ausgabe, *map and plates, half morocco, Leipz.* 1886 — Christmann, Oceanien und Australien, 2 vol. *ib.* 1870-73 ; and others (6)

367 Lang (J. D.) Transportation and Colonization, *half morocco*, 1837 —The Emigrant's Guide to Australia, *n. d.*—The Prisoners of Australia, 1841—Prout (J. S.) Illustrated Handbook of the Voyage to Australia—Ewan (Jas.) Geography of the Australian Colonies, *maps, Sydney*, 1854 (5)

368 La Pilorgerie (J. de) Histoire de Botany Bay, *Paris, Paulin*, 1836—De Doncourt (A. S.) L'Australie, *Lille, Lefort, s. d.*— Océanie, par G. L. D. de Rienzi, 3 vol. *numerous illustrations, Paris, Didot*, 1836—Salvado (R.) Mémoires sur l'Australie, *ib.* 1854 ; and others (8)

369 La Pérouse (J. F. G. de) Voyage Round the World, 1785-88, 3 vol. *maps and plates, half calf*, 1807—Dillon (Capt. P.) Narrative of a Voyage in the South Seas to ascertain the actual Fate of La Pérouse's Expedition, 2 vol. *map and frontispieces, boards, uncut*, 1829 (5)

370 La Pérouse (J. F. G. de) Voyage Round the World, 1785-88,
3 vol. *portrait, maps and plates, calf (broken)*, *J. Johnson*, 1798
—Voyage in Search of La Pérouse by Labillardière, 2 vol.
maps and plates, calf, *J. Stockdale*, 1800 (5)

371 Lee (Mrs. R.) Adventures in Australia, 1853—Butler (Sam.)
Handbook for Australian Emigrants, *map*, *Glasgow*, 1839—
The New Zealanders, *Nattali*, 1847—Meredith (Mrs. Ch.)
Notes and Sketches of New South Wales, 1844 ; &c. (6)

372 Leguat (Fr.) Voyages and Avantures en deux Isles Desertes des
Indes Orientales, 2 vol. in 1, *maps and plates, old calf,
D. Mortier*, 1721—Les Entretiens des Voyageurs sur la Mer,
Cologne, P. Marteau, 1683 ; and others (4)

373 Leichardt (Dr. L.) Journal of an Overland Expedition from
Moreton Bay to Port Essington, 1844-5, *plates, cloth, Boone,*1847

374 Leichardt (Dr. L.) Journal of an Overland Expedition in Australia
from Moreton Bay to Port Essington, 1844-5, *plates, cloth,
Boone*, 1847—Hood (T. H.) Notes of a Cruise in H.M. Fawn
in the Western Pacific in 1862, *plates, cloth, Edinb.* 1863—
Cruise of H.M. Galatea under the Duke of Edinburgh, by
Milner and Brierly, *plates, cloth, Allen and Co.* 1869 (3)

375 Leichardt (Dr. L.) Tagebuch einer Landreise in Australien,
1844-5 aus dem Englischen von E. A. Zuchold, *Halle*, 1851 ;
Briefe an Seine Angehörigen, *portrait and map, half morocco,
Hamb.* 1881—Hunter's Historische Nachrichten von Port
Jackson and Norfolk's-Insel, aus dem Englishchen, 2 vol. *por-
trait and plates, Nürnb.* 1794 ; and others (6)

376 Leigh (W. H.) Reconnoitering Voyages, Travels and Adventures
in the New Colonies of South Australia, &c. 1836-38, *half
morocco gilt* *Smith, Elder*, 1839

377 Leigh (W. H.) Reconnoitering Voyages and Travels, *second edition,
numerous engravings, tree-calf extra, m. c. by Riviere* 1840

378 Letter from Sydney, edited by R. Gouger, *map* 1829

379 Lhotsky (Dr. John) Present State and Future Prospects of New
South Wales, *Sydney*, 1835—Atkinson (Jas.) State of Agriculture and Grazing in New South Wales, *coloured plates*, 1826

380 Lhotsky (Dr. John) Journey from Sydney to the Australian
Alps, 1834 *Sydney*, 1835

381 Linnean Society of New South Wales (Proceedings), *plates*, vol. I
to IV, *half calf* *Sydney (published for the Society)*, 1877-9

382 Lloyd (G. Thomas) Thirty-Three Years in Tasmania and Victoria,
map, 1862—Martineau (John) Letters from Australia, 1869—
Westgarth (Wm.) Australia Felix, *Edinb.* 1848—Mann (W.)
Six Years in the Australian Provinces, *map*, 1839; and
others (6)

383 Logan (J. R.) Languages of the Indian Archipelago ; a System
of Classification and Orthography for Comparative Vocabu-
laries ; on the Generation and Developments of Languages,
cloth *Singapore, Free Press, n. d.*

384 Lunatic Asylums in New South Wales (Report on), by F. Norton Manning, *plans, half morocco*
     imp. 8vo. Sydney, T. Richards, 1868

385 Lyne (Ch.) The Industries of New South Wales, *plates, imp. 8vo, Sydney,* 1882—Heaton (J. H.) Australian Dictionary of Dates and Men of the Time, *ib.* 1879—Fry (Rev. H. Ph.) System of Penal Discipline, 1850 ; and others   (5)

386 Lyne (Ch.) The Industries of New South Wales, *plates,* 1882—Griffin (G. W.) New South Wales, her Commerce and Resources, 1888—Richards (Thos.) New South Wales in 1881, *Sydney*—Transactions of the Philosophical Society of New South Wales, 1862-5, *ib.* ; and others   (12)

387 [Macarthur (Jas.)] New South Wales, its Present State and Future Prospects, *calf gilt, m. e. by Riviere D. Walther,* 1837

388 Macartney (Jo. Neill) The Bendigo Goldfield Registry, *maps, Melbourne,* 1871—Mines and Mineral Statistics of New South Wales, *plans, Sydney,* 1875 — Mining Surveyors' Reports (Victoria), vol. III, *Melbourne,* 1861—Mining and Mineral Statistics by R. Brough Smith, *red morocco, ib.* 1866—Austin (J. B.) Mines of South Australia, *Adelaide,* 1863—Stainsfield (C. W.) Australian Tradesmen's Tokens, 1883 ; and others (9)

389 Mc Combie (Hon. T.) History of the Colony of Victoria, *Melbourne,* 1858—Auckland, and the Country adjacent, with Account of the Gold Discovery, *map and frontispiece,* 1853—Sutton (G.) The Culture of the Grape Vine and Orange in Australia and New Zealand, 1843—Jones (Rev. H. B.) Adventures in Australia, 1852-3—Harrison (Rob.) Five Years in South Australia, 1862 ; and others   (8)

390 Mc Coy (Fred.) Prodromous of the Zoology of Victoria, 50 *coloured plates, half morocco imp. 8vo. Melbourne,* 1878

391 Macdonald (D.) Gum Boughs and Wattle Bloom gathered on Australian Hills and Plains, *Cassell*—Hawthorn (J. R. H.) The Pioneer of a Family, 1881—The Boy in the Bush by R. Rowe —Memoir and Journal of Commodore Goodenough, *maps,* 1876 ; and others   (6)

392 Macgillivray (John) Voyage of the Rattlesnake Commanded by Capt. Owen Stanley, including Discoveries and Surveys in New Guinea, the Louisiade Archipelago, &c. *map and plates,* 2 vol. *cloth*   *Boone,* 1852

393 Mackay (Angus) The Sugar Cane in Australia, a Series of Essays upon Cultivation and Manufacture, *half morocco, imp. 8vo, Brisbane, G. Slater,* 1870—Another Edition, *fully illustrated, cloth, imp. 8vo, Sydney* (1883)   (2)

394 Mackenzie (Rev. D.) The Emigrant's Guide to South Australia, *W. S. Orr,* 1845—Butler (Sam) Hand-Book for Australian Emigrants, *map, Glasgow,* 1839—Gouger (R.) South Australia in 1837, *Harvey and Darton,* 1838—Harrison (R.) Colonial Sketches or Five Years in South Australia, 1862 ; and others   (8)

395 Mc Kinlay (John) Journal of Exploration in the Interior of Australia (Burke Relief Expedition), 3 *maps loose in case, half bound, Melbourne, Bailliere* (1861) ; Davis (John) Tracks of Mc Kinlay and Party across Australia, edited by W. Westgarth, *coloured plates (wants map), half calf gilt*
Sampson Low, 1863

396 Macleay (Hon. Wm.) Descriptive Catalogue of Australian Fishes, 2 vol. *cloth* *Sydney, F. W. White*, 1881

397 Maclehose. Picture of Sydney and Strangers' Guide to New South Wales for 1838, *map and woodcuts on paper of various tints, cloth, very scarce* 12mo. *Sydney, J. Maclehose*, 1838

398 Maclehose. Picture of Sydney in 1838, *map and woodcut views on various coloured paper, half morocco* *ib.* 1838

399 Maconochie (Capt.) Australiana. Thoughts on Convict Management, and other Subjects connected with the Australian Penal Colonies, *calf gilt by Riviere* *J. W. Parker*, 1839

400 Major (R. H.) Discoveries of Prince Henry the Navigator, and their Results, *portraits, maps, &c. cloth* *Sampson Low*, 1877

401 Mann (W.) Six Years' Residence in the Australian Provinces ending in 1839, *map, calf gilt*, 1839—Hursthouse (Ch.) An Account of New Plymouth, the Garden of New Zealand, *map, calf gilt*, 1851—Bonwick (Jas.) Curious Facts of Old Colonial Days, *half morocco*, 1870 (3)

401* Maori Mementos, a Series of Addresses presented by the Native People to Sir George Grey, with Introductory Remarks, explanatory Notes, a small Collection of Laments, &c. by C. O. B. Davis, *cloth* *Auckland, Williamson and Wilson*, 1855

402 Map of the Settled Districts around Melbourne, with Book of Reference, *Melbourne*, 1853—How to Settle in Victoria, *ib.* 1855—Plunkett (J. H.) Australian Magistrates' Pocket Book, *Sydney*, 1859—Mackenzie (Rev. D.) The Gold Digger, *map*, (1853)—Gazetteer of New South Wales, 1866 ; and others (10)

403 Mariner (Wm.) Account of the Natives of the Tonga Islands, with a Grammar and Vocabulary of their Language by J. Martin, *frontispiece*, 2 vol. *half calf*, 1817—Lebas (Rev. C. W.) Life of Bishop Middleton, *portrait*, 2 vol. *half bound*, 1831 (4)

404 Markham (Comm. A. H.) Cruise of the Rosario amongst the New Hebrides and Santa Cruz Islands, *map and illustrations, cloth*, 1873—Goldsmid (Col. Sir Fr. J.) Telegraph and Travel, *map and illustrations, cloth*, 1874—Leathes (Edm.) An Actor Abroad, *cloth*, 1880 (3)

405 Marshall (W. B.) Two Visits to New Zealand in 1834, *frontispiece, half morocco gilt*, 1834—Lang (J. D.) Transportation and Colonization, 1837—Blenkinsop (Dr.) Transport Voyage to the Mauritius and Back, *half bound*, 1851—Ward (John) Information relative to New Zealand, *map*, 1840 ; and others (6)

406 MARTIN (Jas.) The Australian Sketch Book, by the late Chief Justice of N.S.W. *very rare, half morocco* *Sydney*, 1838

407 Martin (R. M.) Statistics of the Colonies of the British Empire, *map and plates, cloth*   imp. 8vo. *Allen and Co.* 1839

408 Martin (S. M. D. M.D.) New Zealand in a Series of Letters, containing an Account of the Country, with Historical Remarks on the Conduct of the Government, &c. *calf gilt, m. e. by Riviere*   *Simmonds and Ward,* 1845

409 May (Sir T. E.) Treatise on the Law, Privileges, Proceedings and Usage of Parliament, *ninth edition, cloth*   1883

410 Melbourne University Calendars from 1858 to 1882, 20 vol. *Melbourne*—Sydney University Calendars, 1852-54, 1860-63, 1866 and 1887, 8 vol. *Sydney*   (28)

411 Melbourne Review (The), vol. I-VII, *half red morocco*   imp. 8vo. *Melbourne, S. Mullen, etc.* 1876-82

412 Melville (H.) Australasia and Prison Discipline, *calf gilt,* 1851— Barker (Lady) Station Amusements in New Zealand, *map and frontispiece,* 1873—Dana (J. D.) Corals and Coral, *map and illustrations, half bound,* 1875—Eden (C. H.) The Fifth Continent, *map, S. P. C. K.*   (4)

413 Mennell (Ph.) Dictionary of Australasian Biography, 1855-1892, *half roan,* 1892—Heaton (J. H.) Australian Dictionary of Dates and Men of the Time, *cloth, Sydney,* 1879   (2)

414 Mennell (Ph.) Dictionary of Australasian Biography, 1855-92, *half bound,* 1892—Boyd (Mark) Reminiscences of Fifty Years, 1871—Mossmann and Banister, Australia Visited and Revisited, *map,* 1853—Howe (Edw.) Roughing it in Van Diemen's Land, *Strahan, n. d. ;* and others   (6)

415 Meredith (Mrs. Charles) My Home in Tasmania, during a Residence of nine years, *woodcuts,* 2 vol. *green cloth*   *J. Murray,* 1852

416 Meredith (L. A.) Over the Straits, a Visit to Victoria, *illustrated*   1861

417 Merivale (H.) Lectures on Colonization and Colonies, delivered at Oxford, 1839, '40, '41, *cloth*   *Longmans,* 1861

418 Meyer (H. A. E.) Vocabulary of the Language Spoken by the Aborigines of South Australia, preceded by a Grammar, *half morocco*   *Adelaide, J. Allen,* 1843

419 Meyer (H. A. E.) Another copy, *half bound*   *ib.* 1843

420 Michie (Sir Arch.) Readings in Melbourne, 1879—St. Johnston (Alfred) Camping among Cannibals, 1883—Senior (Wm.) Travel and Trout in the Antipodes, *Melbourne,* 1880— Australia in 1866 by a Clergyman, 1868 ; and others   (7)

421 Mineral Products of New South Wales by Harrie Wood ; Notes on the Geology of New South Wales, by C. S. Wilkinson, &c. *Sydney,* 1882—Reports of Geological Explorations during 1871-2, *maps, Wellington,* 1872—Clarke (Rev. W. B.) Recent Geological Discoveries in Australasia, *Sydney,* 1861 ; and other Pamphlets   (20)

D

422 Mitchell (Maj. T. L.) Three Expeditions into the Interior of Eastern Australia, &c. *second edition, maps and plates (stained)*, 2 vol. *half bound*   *Boone*, 1839

423 Mitchell (Maj. T. L.) Three Explorations into the Interior of Eastern Australia, Australia Felix and New South Wales, *numerous illustrations*, 2 vol. *tree-calf extra, m. e. by Rivière*
                                                                        Boone, 1838

424 Mitchell. Journal of an Expedition into the Interior of Tropical Australia, *numerous plates, tree-calf extra, m. e. by Rivière*
                                                                        Longmans, 1848

425 Moore (G. Fletcher) Descriptive Vocabulary of the Language in Common Use amongst the Aborigines of Western Australia, *half bound*   *Lond. W. Orr*, 1842

426 Moore (G. F.) Vocabulary of the Native Dialect of Western Australia   1842

427 Moresby (Capt. John) Discoveries and Surveys in New Guinea and Polynesia, *maps and plates, cloth, J. Murray*, 1876— Glimpses of Life in Victoria, by a Resident, *plates, cloth*, 1872 —Boddam-Whetham (J. W.) Pearls of the Pacific, *illustrated, cloth*, 1876   (3)

428 Moser (Th.) Mahoe Leaves, Sketches of New Zealand, *Wellington, N. Z.* 1863 — Zillmann (Rev. J. H. L.) Past and Present Australian Life, 1889—The Aborigines and the Chinese in Australia ; and others   (17)

429 Moss (Fr. J.) Through Atolls, and Islands in the Great South Sea, *plates, Sampson Low*, 1889—M'Farlane (Rev. S.) Story of the Lifu Mission, *map and plates*, 1873— Heywood (B. A.) Travels and Excursions in Victoria, Tasmania, New South Wales, etc., *n. d.* ; and others   (6)

430 Mudie. The Picture of Australia [by R. Mudie], *half morocco*
                                                                        1829

431 Mudie (Jas.) Picture of Australia, *map, Whittaker*, 1829—Recollections of Seven Years Residence at the Mauritius, 1830— Wathen (G. H.) Golden Colony, or Victoria in 1854—Capper (H.) South Australia, *map*, 1838 ; and others   (6)

432 Mudie (Jas.) Felonry of New South Wales, *plan of Sydney, calf gilt, m. e. by Riviere*   *Printed for the Author*, 1837

433 Mudie (Jas.) Felonry of New South Wales, another copy, *map*
                                                                        1837

434 Mueller (Baron von) Fragmenta Phytographiæ Australiæ, *plates*, 4 vol. *cloth*   *Melbourne*, 1858-64

435 Mueller. Select Extra-tropical Plants, *Sydney*, 1881—The Same, Definitions of Rare, or hitherto undescribed Australian Plants, *Melbourne*, 1855—Schomburgk (Dr. R.) Catalogue of Plants under Cultivation in the Government Botanic Garden, Adelaide, *Adelaide*, 1878—Thomson (G. M.) The Ferns and Fern Allies of New Zealand, *Melbourne*, 1882 ; and others (8)

436 Mueller (Baron F. von) Select Extra-Tropical Plants (New South Wales Edition), *half calf, Sydney, T. Richards*, 1881—The same (New Victorian Edition), *cloth, Melbourne, Jo. Ferres*, 1885 (2)

437 Mundy (Lt. Col. G. C.) Our Antipodes ; Residence and Rambles in the Australian Colonies, *plates*, 3 vol. *calf gilt, m. e. by Rivière*   *R. Bentley*, 1852

438 Mundy (G. Ch.) Our Antipodes ; Residence and Rambles in the Australian Colonies, *plates*, 3 vol. *cloth*   *ib.* 1852

439 Mundy (E. C.) Wanderungen in Australien   *Leipz.* 1856

440 Murchison (Sir R. I.) Life, based on his Letters and Journals, by A. Geikie, *portraits and woodcuts*, 2 vol. 1875—Denison (Sir W.) Varieties of Vice-Regal Life, *map.* 2 vol. 1870   (4)

441 Murray (Rev. T. B.) Pitcairn, 1854—The Draper in Australia, 1856—Weale's Guide to Australia—Australia (by F. Angas) *S. P. C. K.* ; and others   (8)

442 Murray (Rev. A. W.) Forty Years Mission Work in Polynesia and New Guinea, 1835-75, *map and frontispiece*   1876

443 Napier (Col. C. J.) Colonization particularly in Southern Australia, *half morocco, Boone,* 1835—Widowson (H.) Present State of Van Diemen's Land, *map*, 1829—Chamerovzow (L. A.) The New Zealand Question and the Rights of Aborigines, *half morocco, T. Newby,* 1848   (3)

444 Napier (Col. C. J.) Colonization, particularly in Southern Australia, *half bound*   *Boone*, 1835

445 National Banquet at Sydney, 17th July, 1856, to Celebrate Responsible Government in New South Wales, edited by R. Thompson, *Sydney, T. Daniel,* 1856—Henderson (Wm.) Christianity and Modern Thought, *Ballarat,* 1861 — Musgrave (Capt. Thos.) Castaway on the Auckland Isles (Wreck of the "Grafton ") *map, Melbourne,* 1865— Gurner (H. F.) Chronicle of Port Phillip, 1770-1840, *ib.* 1876—Clayden (A.) The England of the Pacific (New Zealand), *plates,* 1879—Bathgate (John) New Zealand, its Resources and Prospects, *map and illustrations,* 1880   (6)

446 New Holland (History of) from its first Discovery in 1616 to the Present Time, *maps,* 1787—The Public Surveys of New South Wales, *Sydney,* 1866— Earl (G. Windsor) Handbook for Colonists in Tropical Australia, 1882   (3)

447 New Holland. History of New Holland from its first Discovery in 1616 to the Present Time ; with account of its Produce and Inhabitants, &c. 2 *charts, calf gilt*   *J. Stockdale,* 1787

448 New South Wales, Geographical Memoirs on, by various Hands, edited by Barron Field, *map and plates, boards, uncut J. Murray,* 1825

449 New South Wales. Official Report of the National Australasian Convention Debates, March-April, 1891, *red morocco gilt roy. 8vo. Sydney,* 1891

450 New South Wales and Port Phillip General Post Office Directory for 1839, printed and published by permission of Jas. Raymond, Esq. *half bound, very scarce 12mo. Sydney, J. Maclehose,* 1839

451 New South Wales Calendar and General Post Office Directory for 1835, 1836, and 1837, 3 vol. *half bound*   *Sydney*

452 New South Wales Pocket Almanack for 1820, published under the Sanction of his Excellency the Governor and Commander-in Chief, *half bound*, VERY RARE *Sydney, G. Howe*, 1820

453 New South Wales Racing Calendar. "The Era" Racing Calendar, or Colonial "Ruff" for 1858, edited by J. Boyd-Price, *portrait of the racehorse Dora, half morocco, very scarce Sydney* (1858)

454 New South Wales Stud Book, containing Pedigrees of Race Horses, 3 vol. (*not uniform*) VERY RARE *Sydney*, 1859-68-73

455 New Zealand Journal of Science (The), vol. I—II, *half morocco roy. 8vo. Dunedin, N. Z.* 1882-5

456 New Zealand Institute Transactions and Proceedings, 1870, vol. III, *Wellington*—Geological Magazine, vol. VIII, 1871—Royal Society of Van Diemen's Land, Papers and Proceedings, vol I. *Tasmania*, 1851—Geographical Society of Australasia. Proceedings, vol. I, and "Special Volume," *Sydney*, 1885, &c. (11)

457 New Zealand Portfolio (The) embracing a series of Papers on Subjects of Importance to the Colonists, conducted by H. S. Chapman, *calf gilt by Rivière* *Smith, Elder*, 1843

458 New Zealand Pilot, compiled by Capt. G. H. Richards, and F. J. Evans, 1859—Shillinglaw (J. J.) Historical Records of Port Phillip, 1879—Handbook to Sydney and Suburbs (*wants map*), *n. d. ;* and others (6)

459 Nicholas (J. L.) Voyage to New Zealand, 1814-5, 2 vol. *maps and plates (stained), half calf* 1817

460 Nicolay (Rev. C. G.) Handbook of Western Australia, *Perth*, 1880—New South Wales Constitution Bill. Speeches in the Legislative Assembly, *Sydney*, 1853—The Riverine Question, Speeches in the Legislative Assembly of New South Wales, *top of title torn, Melbourne*, 1864—Conigrave (J. F.) South Australian Handbook, *plates*, 1886 ; and others (7)

461 Nicols (Arthur) Wild Life and Adventure in the Australian Bush, 2 vol. *illustrated, R. Bentley*, 1887—Pyne (Rev. A.) Reminiscences of Colonial Life, 1875—Chalmers and Gill, Work and Adventure in New Guinea, *illustrated, R. T. S. ;* and others (6)

462 Niew Guinea. Ethnographisch en Natuurkundig Onderzocht en Beschreven in 1858, 26 *ethnographic plates and 7 maps, half morocco, Amst. F. Muller*, 1862—Van Der Aa (Robidé) Reizen naar Nederlandsch Nieuw-Guinea, *maps, half morocco, 'S Gravenhage, Mart. Nijhoff*, 1879 (2)

463 Nieuw Guinea. Ethnographisch en Natuurkundig, 26 *plates, and the 7 maps in a separate vol. half morocco, Amst. F. Muller*, 1862—Kolff (D. H.) Reize door Nieuw-Guinea, *map, ib. G. J. A. Bijerinck*, 1828—Modera (J.) Reize naar Nieuw-Guinea, *Haarlem*, 1830—Twee Togten naar de Golf Van Carpentaria (*J. Cartensz*, 1623 ; *J. E. Gonzal*, 1756), *Amst. Schellema*, 1859 (5)

464 Nisbet (Hume) A Colonial Tramp. Travels and Adventures in Australia and New Guinea, 2 vol. *numerous illustrations, cloth Ward and Downey*, 1891

465 Nisbet (Hume). Where Art Begins, *illustrated*, 1892—Life and Nature Studies, 1887—The Jolly Roger—Land of the Hibiscus Blossom, *illustrated*, 1888—The Black Drop, 1891 (5)

466 Notice sur la Transportation à la Guyane Française et à la Nouvelle-Calédonie pour les Années 1880-1, *half morocco* *imp. 8vo. Paris, Imp. Nationale*, 1884

467 Ogle (N.) Colony of Western Australia ; a Manual for Emigrants, *map and plates, tree-calf extra, m. e. by Riviere J. Fraser*, 1839

468 Ogle (N.) The Colony of Western Australia, *map and plates, cloth,* 1839—Sidney (S.) Three Colonies of Australia, *map (in pocket) and illustrations*, 1853 — Finch-Hatton (Hon. H.) Advance Australia ! *plates, cloth*, 1885 (3)

469 O'Hara. History of New South Wales, *calf gilt, m. e.* *Printed for the author*, 1817

470 [O'Hara]. History of New South Wales, *half morocco* *Printed for the author*, 1817

471 Oliver (Alex.) Collection of the Statutes of Practical Utility in Force in New South Wales, from 1824 to date, with Chronological Table and Index, 3 vol. *half law calf* *Sydney, T. Richards*, 1879

472 Oliver (Alex.) Statutes of New South Wales, another copy, 3 vol. *half law calf* *ib.* 1879

QUARTO.

473 Fowles (Joseph) Sydney in 1848, illustrated by Copperplate Engravings of its Principal Streets, Public Buildings, Churches, Chapels, etc. *half morocco, Sydney, J. D. Wall* (1848)

474 Geographical Magazine (The) edited by C. R. Markham, *maps,* vol. I to V, *half morocco, sup. imp. 8vo*, 1874-78—Ocean Highways ; The Geographical Review, edited by C. R. Markham, New Series, vol. 1, 31 *maps, half morocco* *ib.* 1874

475 Giglioli (E. H.) Viaggio intorno al Globo della R. Pirocorvetta Italiana Magenta, 1865-68, *with long descriptions of Australian Colonies, maps and woodcuts, boards, uncut* *Milano*, 1873

476 Grant (Baron) History of Mauritius, *maps, calf*, 1801—Bougainville (Louis de) Voyage round the World, translated by J. R. Foster, *maps*, 1772—Wilson (Capt. J.) Missionary Voyage to the Southern Pacific, *calf (poor copy)*, 1799 (3)

477 Grant (Jas.) Narrative of a Voyage of Discovery performed in H. M. S. The Lady Nelson, 1800-1802, to New South Wales, *maps and plates, half calf* *T. Egerton*, 1803

478 Gray (G. R.) Entomology of Australia in a Series of Monographs, part I (Monograph of the Genus Phasma), 8 *coloured plates, cloth, scarce* *Published by the Author*, 1833

479 Gray (G. R.) Entomology of Australia, part I, another copy (*top margin of title cut off*), *cloth* 1833

480 Heads of the People, an Illustrated Journal of Literature, Whims and Oddities, *numerous humorous and other illustrations,* vol. I-II, in 1 vol. *half bound, very scarce* *Sydney*, 1847-8

481 Henshall (Sam.) Specimens and Parts, containing a History of the County of Kent, a Dissertation on the Laws, &c. *map, half morocco* 1798

482 Hochstetter (Dr. J. Von) New Zealand, its Physical Geography, Geology and Natural History, translated from the German by E. Sauter, *maps and numerous illustrations, cloth*
sup. imp. 8vo. Stuttgart, J. G. Gotta, 1867

483 Hooker (J. D.) The Flora of Australia, its Origin, Affinities and Distribution, *cloth* *L. Reeve,* 1859

484 HUNTER (JOHN) HISTORICAL JOURNAL OF THE TRANSACTIONS AT PORT JACKSON AND NORFOLK ISLAND, with Discoveries made in New South Wales and the Southern Ocean since Phillips's Voyage, *portrait, maps and plates, calf gilt,* FINE COPY *Stockdale,* 1793

485 Hunter (John) Historical Journal, another copy, *margins of title and portrait ink-stained, shabby calf* 1793

486 Huxley (F. H.) Oceanic Hydrozoa, observed during the Voyage of H.M.S. Rattlesnake, 1846-50, *plates, cloth Ray Soc.* 1859

487 Jenner (Edw.) An Inquiry into the Causes and Effects of the Variolæ Vaccinæ, known by the name of the Cow Pox, *second edition,* 4 *coloured plates (Australian facsimile Reprint), half calf Lond.* 1800, *reprinted Sydney, T. Richards,* 1884

488 Journals and Reports of Two Voyages to the Glenelg River and the North-West Coast of Australia, 1863-4 (*reprinted from the Perth Gazette), chart, half morocco*
sm. 4to. Perth (Australia), privately printed by A. Shenton, 1864

489 Kreff (Gerard) The Snakes of Australia, 12 *coloured plates, cloth, very scarce Sydney, T. Richards,* 1869

490 Kreff (Gerard) The Snakes of Australia, another copy, *plain plates, half morocco* 1869

491 Landscape Scenery illustrating Sydney and Port Jackson, N. S. W. 20 *views, oblong, Sydney, John Sands, n. d.—* Willoughby (Howard) Australian Pictures drawn with Pen and Pencil, *cloth, R. T. S.—*Prince Alfred in Victoria, 1868 (3)

492 La Pérouse. Voyage Round the World, 1785-88, 2 vol. *calf,* 1799, *and folio atlas to the French edition—*Voyage in Search of La Pérouse, by Labillardière, 46 *plates, calf (broken),* 1800 (4)

493 La Pérouse (J. F. G. de) Voyage autour du Monde, rédigé par L. A. Milet Mureau, 4 vol. *and folio atlas, Paris,* 1797—Voyage à la Recherche de la Pérouse, par Labillardière, 2 vol. *ib.* 1800 ; together 7 vol. *uniform half morocco*

494 Latrobe (Rev. C. J.) Journal of a Visit to South Africa in 1815 and 1816, *map and coloured plates, boards L. B. Seeley,* 1818

495 Lewin (J. W.) A Natural History of the Lepidopterous Insects of New South Wales, 18 *coloured plates, boards, very rare*
J. H. Bohte, 1822

496 Lindsay (W. Lauder) Contributions to New Zealand Botany, 4 *coloured plates, half morocco Williams and Norgate,* 1868

497 Magnetical and Meteorological Observations Made at the Observatory at Hobarton in Van Diemen Island, and by the Anti-Arctic Naval Expedition, 1841-48, 3 vol. *cloth*
Longmans, 1850-3

498 Major (R. H.) Discovery of Australia by the Portuguese in 1601, 1861—Wilson (J. B.) Report on Lord Howe Island, *maps*, *Sydney*, 1882—Railway Guide to New South Wales, *first and third editions, Sydney*, 1881-6—G. Damm, Clavierschule ; and others (7)

499 Marsden (Wm.) Miscellaneous Works (Polynesian or East-Insular Languages, &c.) *cloth* *Published for the author*, 1834

500 Martin (A. Patchett) Fernshawe, Sketches in Prose and Verse, *illustrated, Griffith and Farran, n. d.*—Lays of To Day, *half morocco, Sydney, G. Robertson*, 1878—New South Wales Railway Guides, *first and third editions*, 1881-86 (4)

501 Martin (R. Montgomery) The British Colonies, their History, Condition and Resources, 3 vol. *numerous maps and plates, half red morocco* *sup. imp. 8vo. Lond. Pub. Co. n. d.*

502 Melbourne Punch (The) vol. I to IV, *half morocco, Melbourne*, 1856-7—The same, April 22, 1875 to Dec. 28, 1876, in 2 vol. *bound, very scarce* (6)

503 Mineral Products of New South Wales, by Harrie Wood ; Notes on the Geology of the Same, by C. S. Wilkinson ; Description of the Minerals of the Same, by A. Livesidge, &c. *in a vol. half morocco* *Sydney, T. Richards*, 1882

504 Mineral Products of New South Wales, by Harrie Wood, &c. another copy as above, *half morocco* *Sydney*, 1882

505 Mueller (Baron Ferd. von) Plants of the Colony of Victoria (Thamiflorae and Lithograms), 2 vol. *plain plates, cloth* *Melbourne, John Ferres*, 1860-65

506 Mueller (Baron Ferd. von) Report on the Forest Resources of Western Australia, 20 *plates, cloth* *L. Reeve*, 1879

507 Myers (Francis) Coastal Scenery, Harbours, Mountains and Rivers of New South Wales, *illustrations by the Heliotype process, morocco* *Sydney, T. Richards*, 1886

508 Nathan (I.) The Southern Euphrosyne, and Australian Miscellany, containing Oriental Moral Tales, with examples of the Native Aboriginal Melodies, set to Music, *cloth* *Whittaker, n. d.*

509 Nathan (I.) Selection of Hebrew Melodies, the Poetry by Lord Byron, *cloth* *n. d.*

510 National Gallery of Victoria. Catalogue of the Statues and Busts in Marble, and Casts, *interleaved throughout with some MS. additions, red morocco, Melbourne, Fergusson and Moore*, 1880

511 Navarrete. Coleccion de los Viajes y Descubrimentos que hicieron por Mar los Espanoles desde fines del Siglo XV Coordinada e illustrada por D. Martin Fernandez de Navarette, segunda edicion, 5 vol. *half morocco, wants vol. III, but has copy of the first edition of the same vol. in calf*
sm. 4to. Madrid, 1858

40

FOLIO.

512 Bauer (Ferdinand) Illustrationes Floræ Novæ Hollandiæ descripsit
R. Brown, 14 *plates in duplicate, plain and coloured (and 2 duplicate coloured plates), half morocco*   *imp. fol.* 1813

513 Blaeu's Atlas. ATLAS MAJOR, sive Cosmographia Blaviana,
numerous coloured maps, 11 vol. *vellum gilt, imp. fol. Amst.* 1762

514 BENTLEY MYSTERY (THE). Papers relating to the Bentley
Mystery (T. C. Bentley and Anonymous Letters), New South
Wales, *cloth*   *Sydney,* 1862

515 BIGGE. Report of the Commissioner of Inquiry into the State
of the Colony of New South Wales, 1822

516 BOUGAINVILLE (BARON DE) JOURNAL DU NAVIGATION AUTOUR
DU GLOBE, de la Fregate "La Thetis" et de la Corvette
"l'Espérance," 2 vol. 4to, *of Text and 2 folio atlases of maps,
views, Natural History subjects (the latter coloured), &c. half red
morocco gilt, g. e.*   *Paris,* 1837

517 Brown (J. C.) The Forest Flora of South Australia, *finely coloured
plates,* parts 1-7   *atlas fol. Adelaide,* 1882, &c.

518 CARICATURES. A Collection of 60 Coloured Political Caricatures
by W. Heath, H. B., R. Seymour, Cruikshank and others,
neatly mounted in a vol. and bound in half russia

519 Colonial Gazette (The) June-Dec. 1839, 1840, 1842, 1844 and
1846, 5 vol. *half bound*—Australian Churchman, vol. III-IV,
half bound, Sidney, 1877-9—Church of England Messenger,
Jan. 18, 1877; Dec. 2, 1878, in 1 vol. *half bound, Melbourne*   (8)

520 CONVICTS. Report from the Select Committee on TRANS-
PORTATION, *half morocco*   1838

521 DARLING. Papers relating to the Conduct and Recall of Sir
Chas. Darling, Governor of Victoria, 3 vol.   1835-67

522 EDINBURGH (DUKE OF). Full Report laid before Parliament of
the Attempted Assassination of the Duke of Edinburgh

523 ELLIOT (D. G.) MONOGRAPH OF THE PARADISEIDÆ, or Birds of
Paradise, complete in 7 parts, 37 *beautifully coloured plates*
     atlas fol. 1873

524 Empire (The) Daily Journal of News, Politics and Commerce,
from Jan. 21, 1851 to July 31, 1851, in 1 vol. *half bound*
     Sydney

525 FITZGERALD (R. D.) AUSTRALIAN ORCHIDS, vol. I, *numerous
beautifully coloured plates, half morocco*
     imp. fol. Sydney, T. Richards, 1882

526 Fitzgerald (R. D.) Another copy, *half morocco*   1882

527 Fitzgerald (R. D.) Another copy, vol. I in 7 parts, and vol. II,
parts 1-2   1882-5

528 GARDINER THE BUSHRANGER, New South Wales (all Parliamentary Papers relating to)   1867-75

529 Gould (John) Monograph of the Macropodidæ, or Family of
Kangaroos, 2 parts, 30 *finely coloured plates imp. fol.* 1841-2

530 Gould (John) THE BIRDS OF NEW GUINEA, and the Adjacent Papuan Islands, parts 1-12, *numerous finely coloured plates, boards*
imp. fol. 1875-84

531 GOULD (JOHN) THE BIRDS OF AUSTRALIA, the Gosford copy, 7 vol. *original subscriber's copy, whole bound green morocco extra,* and SUPPLEMENT, parts 1, 2, 4 and 5, *upwards of* 600 *finely coloured plates* *imp. fol.* 1848-70

532 Gould (John) THE MAMMALS OF AUSTRALIA, 3 vol. *original subscriber's copy,* 182 *finely coloured plates, whole bound green morocco extra* *imp. fol.* 1863

533 Gully (John) New Zealand Scenery, 15 *chromo-lithographs after original water-colour drawings, with descriptive text by Dr. Julius von Hirst, cloth* *atlas fol.* Dunedin, N. Z. 1877

534 Gully (John) Another copy, *loose in cloth portfolio* 1877

535 Harris (John) Complete Collection of Voyages and Travels, 2 vol. *numerous maps and plates, calf (broken)* 1744

536 HARVEY'S AUSTRALIAN ALGÆ. A Collection of 513 dried Specimens of Australian Seaweeds, in 6 vol. *mounted (with MS. lists), half morocco* *imp. fol.*

537 Hastings (T.) Vestiges of Antiquity, a Series of (12) Etchings of the Ancient Monastery of St. Augustine, the Cathedral, &c. of Canterbury, *half morocco* *imp. fol.* 1813

538 Herrera (Ant. de) India Occidentalis. Niewe Werelt anders ghenaempt West Indien ; Ordonnez, Beschryvinghe van West Indien ; Le Maire, Spieghel de Australische Navigatie, &c. *maps, portrait of Le Maire and plates, vellum*
Amst. M. Colijn, 1622

539 Illustrated Sydney News, Jan. 3 - June 20, 1891 (*some leaves damaged by nail*)—The Australian Irrigation Colonies, *illustrated*—Bell's Chronological Tables, 1842 (3)

540 Ireland. Special Commission Act, 1888. Reprint of the Shorthand Notes of the Speeches, Proceedings and Evidence taken before the Commissioners (with Index) (12)

541 Kircherus (Athanasius) Mundus Sutteraneus in XII Libros digestus, 2 vol. in 1, *maps and plates, stamped pigskin binding*
Amst. Jansson, 1678

542 Lewin (J. W.) Natural History of the Birds of New South Wales, 26 *finely coloured plates, half morocco* 1822

543 LYCETT (JAS.) VIEWS IN AUSTRALIA, or New South Wales and Van Diemen's Land delineated, 50 *fine coloured plates and map of Van Diemen's Land, wants map of New South Wales, half bound* *oblong.* 1824

THIRD DAY'S SALE.

LOT 544.

PALMER (Rev. T. J.) Narrative of the Sufferings of T. J. Palmer and W. Skirving during a Voyage to New South Wales, 1794, on board the "Surprise" Transport, *Camb.* 1797—Shearston (J. S.) H.M.S. "Nelson," an Account of her first Commission on the Australian Station, *Sydney,* 1885 ; *all half bound* (3)

545   PAMPHLETS RELATING TO THE AUSTRALIAN COLONIES, *some scarce* *a large parcel*

546   Parbury's Oriental Herald and Colonial Intelligencer, British Indian Presidencies and the Eastern Nations, 2 vol. (*some leaves soiled*), *calf* *Parbury and Co.* 1838

547   Parkes (Sir H.) Speeches on the Public Affairs of New South Wales, 1848-74, *cloth,* 1876—Westwood (J. O.) Journal of Eight Years Itinerancy in Victoria, New South Wales, etc. *wants portrait, Melbourne,* 1865—Adderley (Rt. Hon. Sir C. B.) Review of Colonial Policy, 1869 (3)

548   Patchett Martin (A.) Australia and the Empire, *Edinb.* 1889— Coo-éé, Tales of Australian Life by Australian Ladies, edited by Mrs. Patchett Martin, *n. d.* — Barker (Lady) Station Amusements in New Zealand, 1873 — Buchanan (D.) An Australian Orator, 1886 ; *and others* (6)

549   Paterson (G.) History of New South Wales, from its Discovery to the Present, *map and plates, half bound* *Newcastle-upon-Tyne, n. d.*

550   Patteson (J. C. *Missionary Bishop of the Melanesian Islands*) Life by C. M. Yonge, 2 vol. 2 *portraits, half calf, antique style* *Macmillan,* 1874

551   Peter Possum's Portfolio *Sydney, n. d.*

552   Petre (Hon. H. W.) Acccount of the Settlements of the New Zealand Company, *map, calf gilt, Smith, Elder,* 1841—Yate (Rev. Wm.) Account of New Zealand, *portrait and plates, tree calf gilt, by Rivière, Seeley,* 1835—Heaphy (Ch.) Narrative of a Residence in various Parts of New Zealand, *tree calf, Smith, Elder,* 1842 (3)

553 Phillip (Gov. Arthur) Voyage to Botany Bay, &c. *third edition, portrait, map and plate, old calf* imp. 8vo. *Stockdale,* 1790

554 Phillip (Gov. Arthur) Voyage to Botany Bay, &c. *third edition,* another copy, *calf extra, m. e. by Riviere* imp. 8vo. 1790

555 Polack (J. S.) Manners and Customs of the New Zealanders, 2 vol. *map and woodcuts, calf gilt, by Riviere,* 1840 — The same, New Zealand in 1831-7, 2 vol. *map and plates, half bound, R. Bentley,* 1838 (4)

556 Polack (J. S.) New Zealand, Travels and Adventures, 1831-37, 2 vol. *map and plates, tree-calf extra, m. e. by Riviere, Bentley,* 1838

557 Polehampton (Rev. A.) Kangaroo Land, 1862 — Kennedy (E. B.) Four Years in Queensland, *map,* 1870 — Bush Wanderings of a Naturalist, 1861 — Benton (R. P.) Creoles and Coolies, 1859 ; and others (10)

558 Powell (Rev. J. G.) Narrative of a Voyage to Swan River, with an Account of that Settlement, *map, calf gilt, by Riviere*
J. C. Westley, 1831

559 Power (W. Tyrone) Sketches in New Zealand with Pen and Pencil, 1846-48, *numerous illustrations, cloth* Longmans, 1849

560 Power (W. Tyrone) Another copy, *tinted plates and woodcuts, tree-calf extra, m. e. by Riviere* ib. 1849

561 Praed (Mrs. Campbell) Romance of a Station, 2 vol. *Trischler, n. d.*—The Head Station, 3 vol. 1885—Gold Hunter's Adventures, *Boston,* 1864—Grif by B. L. Fargeon, 2 vol. ; and others (11)

562 Praed (Mrs. Campbell) The Bond of Wedlock—His Natural Life, 3 vol.—John Bull and his Island ; and other Novels, &c. (14)

563 Pratt (Rev. G.) Grammar and Dictionary of the Samoan Language, *second edition, Trübner,* 1878 — New and Complete Manual of Maori Conversation by S. A. *Wellington, N. Z.* 1885—Williams (W.) Dictionary of the New Zealand Language and a Concise Grammar *Paihia C. M. Society,* 1844 (3)

564 Prichard (J. C.) Natural History of Man, FIRST EDITION, *coloured and plain illustrations and woodcuts (no maps), half calf*
H. Baillière, 1843

565 QUIR (CAPT. PEDRO FERNANDEZ DE) RELACION DE UN MEMO- RIAL A SU MAGESTAD SOBRE LA POBLACION Y DESCU- BRIMIENTO DE LA QUARTA PARTE DEL MUNDO AUSTRIALIE INCOGNITA, su gran Riqueza y fertilidad (4 *leaves), plain top margins of first and last leaves neatly mended, red morocco extra* sm. 4to. *Pamplona por Carlos de Labayen,* 1610

₊ The first account of the Discovery of Australia. "The only copy in existence."—(J. H. H.)

566 Quir (Capt. Pedro Fernandez de) COPIE DE LA REQUESTE PRE- SENTEE AU ROY D'ESPAGNE PAR LE CAPT. PIERRE FER- DINAND DE QUIR, sur la descouverte de la cinquiesme Partie du monde appellee la terre Australles, incogneuë, e des grandes richesses, et fertilité d'icelle, *old red morocco extra, bound by Bedford* *Paris, s. nom. imp.* 1617

₊ Extremely rare, the first French Translation of the rare Spanish Original of 1610.

567   Quir (Capt. Pedro Fernandez de) TERRA AUSTRALIS INCOGNITA, or a New Southerne Discoverie containing a fifth Part of the World, LATELY FOUND OUT BY F. DE QUIR, a Spanish Capitaine, *never before published, half bound*
                                     sm. 4to. For John Hodgetts, 1617
   ₊ Exceedingly rare, being the first English Book on Australia.

568   Quir. Account of a Memorial presented to his Majesty by Capt. De Quir, translated from the Spanish with Notice (and fac-simile reprint of the rare original), by W. A. Duncan, *half morocco   sm. 4to. Sydney, T. Richards*, 1874

569   [Raymond (Jas.)] New South Wales Calendar (The) and General Post Office Directory for 1832, *map, half morocco*
                              Sydney, Stephens and Stokes, 1832
   ₊ Very rare, being the earliest Directory and Road Book of the Colony.

570   Raynal (F. E.) Les Naufragés, ou Vingt Mois sur un Récif des Iles Auckland, *récit authentique, numerous illustrations, half morocco   imp. 8vo. Paris, Hachette*, 1870

571   Raynal (F. E.) Les Naufragés, ou Vingt Mois sur un Récif des Iles Auckland, *récit authentique, 4ᵉ édition, numerous illustrations, half morocco, g. e.   imp. 8vo. ib.* 1877

572   Read (C. Rudston) What I Heard, Saw and Did at the Australian Gold Fields, *coloured views, cloth, Boone*, 1853 — Burton (W. W.) State of Religion and Education in New South Wales, *map, cloth*, 1840—Something to his Advantage, an Australian Christmas Serial, *plates, Sydney, n. d. ;* &c.   (6)

573   Reid (G. H.) Essay on New South Wales, *cloth, imp. 8vo, Sydney*, 1876—Brassey's Tahiti, *photos*, 1882—Punch Staff Papers, *Sydney*, 1872—Barton (G. B.) Poets and Prose Writers of New South Wales, *ib.* 1866 ; and others   (6)

574   Reid (G. H.) Essay on New South Wales, *ib.* 1876—The Australian Reader (Memorable Historic Events), *Melbourne*, 1882 —Young (J. S.) Victorian Charades, *ib.* 1870—Parkes (Sir H.) Federal Government of Australasia, Speeches, *Sydney*, 1890 ; and others   (6)

575   Reid (Thos.) Two Voyages to New South Wales and Van Diemen's Land, *tree-calf gilt, m. e. by Riviere Longmans*, 1822

576   Reid (Thos.) Two Voyages to New South Wales and Van Diemen's Land, *calf   ib.* 1822

577   Report of the Capital Punishment Commission, *Sydney, P. Richards*, 1868—Cox (S. S.) Memorial Addresses on the Life and Character of, *portrait, morocco, Washington*, 1890— The Matrimonial Causes Act, 1873, edited by J. Harvie-Finklater, 1878 ; and others   (18)

578   Report of the Parliamentary Select Committee on Aboriginal Tribes, *half morocco*, 1837—Lang (G. S.) Aborigines of Australia, *half morocco, Melbourne*, 1865—Allwood (Rev. R.) Lectures on the Papal Claim of Jurisdiction, *half morocco, Sydney*, 1843—Vaughan (Archbp.) Pastoral and Speeches, *morocco extra (presentation copy), Sydney*, 1860 ; and others (6)

579 Richards (Thos.) An Epitome of the Official History of New South Wales from 1788 to 1883, compiled chiefly from Official and Parliamentary Records, *green morocco gilt, m. e.*
imp. 8vo. Sydney, 1883

580 Ritchie (Leitch) History of the Oriental Nations, 2 vol. 1848— Mills (A.) Colonial Constitutions, 1856—Bannister (S.) Humane Policy; or, Justice to the Aborigines, 1830 ; and others (7)

581 Roberts (Jane) Two Years at Sea ; the Narrative of a Voyage to the Swan River and Van Diemen's Land, 1829-31 ; *frontispiece, tree-calf extra, m. e. by Riviere* *R. Bentley*, 1834

582 Robertson (G. W.) Rise, Progress and Plans of the South Australian Protestant Emigration Community, *map*, 1837—Stewart's Special Settlement at the Bay of Plenty, New Zealand, 1880 —Bell (J. W.) Early Experiences of Colonial Life in South Australia, *Adelaide*, 1878—Daintree (R.) Queensland, Australia, *map, Cornhill, G. Street, n. d. ;* and others (7)

583 Rochfort (John) Adventures of a Surveyor in New Zealand and the Australian Gold Diggings, *frontispiece and illustrated title, D. Bogue*, 1853—Lectures on Gold for the Instruction of Emigrants to Australia, 1852—Mason (Cyrus) An Australian Story Book, *illustrated, Melbourne*, 1872—Fowler (Frank) Southern Lights and Shadows ; Notes of Three Years in Australia, 1859 (4)

584 Roggeveen (Jac.) Dagverhaal der Ont-dekkings—Reis met de Schepen den Arend, &c. en 1721-22, *map, Middelburg*, 1838-- Twee Togten naar de Golf van Carpentaria (J. Cartense, 1623 ; J. E. Gonzal, 1756), *Amst. Scheltema*, 1859—Nederlandsche Reizen, 13th *vol. plates, Amst.* 1787 ; and 1 other (4)

585 Ross (Capt. Sir J. C.) Voyage of Discovery and Research in the Southern and Antarctic Regions, 1839-43, 2 vol. *maps, plates and woodcuts, cloth* *J. Murray*, 1847

586 Rovings in the Pacific 1837 to 1849, with a Glance at California, 2 vol. *coloured plates, half morocco*, 1851— Picture of Australia, by R. Mudie, *map, calf*, 1829—Whately (Archbp.) Remarks on Transportation, *calf*, 1834 (4)

587 Rowcroft (Ch.) The Bushranger : or, Van Diemen's Land (Second Series of "The Tales of the Colonies"), 3 vol. *calf gilt*, 1851

588 Rowcroft (Ch.) An Emigrant in Search of a Colony, 1851— Mitchell (Sir T. L.) The Australian Geography, *map, Sydney*, 1851—Sutherland (A. and G.) History of Australia, 1606-76, *Melbourne*, 1877—The Stranger's Guide to Sydney, *map and cuts, Sydney, J. W. Waugh*, 1861—The New British Province of South Australia, *map and woodcuts, C. Knight*, 1834 ; and others (8)

589 Royal Colonial Institute (Proceedings of the), vol. XII to XXIV, *cloth* 1880-93

590 Royal Geographical Society (Journal of the) from the Commencement to 1880, vol. I to L, with Indexes to vol. I to XXX, and vol. XL to L; Supplementary Papers (1882-5), vol. I, and 2 Catalogues; together 57 vol. 41 *half bound, remainder cloth*, 1830-80; Proceedings, 33 nos. (various) between Nov. 1880 and July 1891

591 ROYAL SOCIETY OF NEW SOUTH WALES. Journal and Proceedings for 1873, 1875 to 1891 (except 1877) and duplicates of vol. X and XIII, *numerous illustrations and maps*
                              Sydney, T. Richards, &c.

592 Rusden (G. W.) Discovery, Survey and Settlement of Port Phillip (and Chronicle of Port Phillip 1770-1840 by H. F. Gurner)   *Melbourne*, 1871-76

593 Rusden (G. W.) History of Australia, 3 vol. *map (with loose leaf of errata in vol. I), cloth   Chapman and Hall*, 1883

594 Rusden (G. W.) History of New Zealand, 3 vol. *map (with 4 leaves of appendix and autograph note in vol. I), cloth ib.* 1883

595 Rusden (G. W.) Aureretanga; Groans of the Maoris, 1888— Bidwill (J. Carne) Rambles in New Zealand, *map*, 1841— Dow (J. L.) The Australian in America, *Melbourne*, 1884; and others   (6)

596 Russell (H. C.) Climate of New South Wales, *Sydney*, 1877— Three Years on the Australian Station, *maps and plates (for private circulation)*, 1868—Stephens (John) History of South Australia, *map*, 1839—Campbell (Wm.) The Crown Lands of Australia, 1855; and others   (7)

597 Russell (H. C.) Climate of New South Wales, *half morocco*, *Sydney, C. Potter*, 1877—Bird (S. D.) Australian Climates and Pulmonary Consumption, *plates*, 1863—Holland (Sir H.) Essays on Scientific and other Subjects, 1862; and others (9)

598 Russell (H. Stuart) Genesis of Queensland, *map and portrait, cloth*
                              imp. 8ro.   Sydney, 1888

599 Sadeur (Jac.) Les Avantures dans la Découverte et le Voyage de la Terre Australe, *Paris, C. Barbin*, 1692—Sadeur, Nouveau Voyage de la Terre Australe, *ib.* 1693

600 Salvado (Mons. D. Rudesino) Memorie Storiche dell' Australia particolarmente della Missione Benedettina di Nuova Norciæ, *map, half morocco, Roma*, 1851—Ule (Dr. Otto) Die neuesten Entdeckungen, in Afrika, Australien, und die arktischen Polarwelt, *maps and illustrations, half morocco, Halle*, 1861 (3)

601 Saunders (T.) Settlement of Port Flinders and the Province of Albert, *maps and views*   1853

602 Savage (John) Some Account of New Zealand, *plates*, 1807— Petre (H. H. W.) Account of the Settlements of the New Zealand Company, *second edition, map*, 1841—Tracts relative to the Aborigines, published by direction of the Meeting for Sufferings, 1838-42—Cunningham (Peter) Hints for Australian Emigrants, 1841; and others   (6)

603 Scratchley (Sir P.) Australian Defences and New Guinea, *portrait and maps*, 1887—Chalmers (Jas.) Pioneering in New Guinea, *map and illustrations by E. Whymper, R. T. S.* 1887—Taylor (Rev. R.) Past and Present of New Zealand, *numerous illustrations*, 1868 (3)

604 Seemann (B.) Viti ; Account of a Government Mission to the Vitian or Fijian Islands, 1860-1, *map and plates, cloth, Camb.* 1862—Grant (A. C.) Bush-Life in Queensland, 2 vol. 1881 (3)

605 Selector's Guide (The) an Explanation of the System of alienating and Leasing Crown Lands in Queensland, *Brisbane*, 1883 —Brown (J. E.) Tree Culture in South Australia, *woodcuts, Adelaide*, 1881—Nilson (Arvid) Timber Trees of New South Wales, *Sydney*, 1884—Warren (W. H.) Strength and Elasticity of New South Wales Timbers of Commercial Value, *ib.* 1887 ; and others (7)

606 Sevarambes (Histoire des) Peuples qui habitent la Terre Australe, 2 vol. in 1, *plates, old calf, Amst. E. Roger*, 1716—Petits Voyages historiques dans l'Asie, l'Afrique, l'Amérique et les Terres Australes par le Baron de M****, 2 vol. 32 *coloured plates, half bound, Paris, Sautin*, 1813 (3)

607 Shaw (Dr. John) Gallop to the Antipodes, *half bound*, 1858—Scherer (John) The Gold Finder of Australia, 28 *plates, half bound, Clarke and Beeton, n. d.*—Rowcroft (John) Tales of the Colonies, 1845—Melbourne in 1869, by S. G. Carter, *map and plates, half bound*, 1870 ; and others (6)

608 Shaw (John) A Tramp to the Diggings in 1852—Jones (Mrs. Henry) Long Years in Australia, 1878—Woolley (John) Lectures delivered in Australia, 1862—Lyra Australis, by C. W. Leakey, 1854 ; and others (6)

609 Shepherd (Thos.) Lectures on Landscape Gardening in Australia
Sidney, 1836

610 Sherer (John) Gold-Finder of Australia, 48 *plates, Clarke, Beeton and Co.*—Whitworth (R. P.) Lost and Found, *half bound, Melbourne*, 1873—Australian Romances, &c. (27)

611 Sherer (John) The Gold Finder of Australia, 28 *engravings, calf gilt, m. e. by Riviere* *n. d.*

612 Shillibeer (Lieut. J.) Narrative of the Briton's Voyage to Pitcairns Island, *plates, Taunton*, 1817—J. Mc Douall Stuart's Explorations Across the Continent of Australia, *with charts, Melbourne*, 1863—D'Albertis (L. M.) Journal of the Expedition for the Exploration of the Fly River, *Sydney*, 1877 ; and others (8)

613 Shipwrecks, &c. The Doddington, The Countess de Bourk, Porpoise and Cato, Capt. Thos. Keith in America, &c. *plates, T. Tegg*—The Maid and the Magpie, Lovel Castle, Children of the Abbey, Story of the Slave, Captive Fair, Father Innocent, Canterbury Tales, the Solemn Warning, The Demon of Venice, *all with coloured plates, Mason and Tegg, in 1 vol. half calf*

614 Shoberl (Fr.) World in Miniature. South Sea Islands, 2 vol. in 1, 26 *coloured plates, cloth* *Ackermann, n. d.*

615 Shortland (Edw.) Maori Religion and Mythology, 1882—Suttor (Geo.) Culture of the Grape Vine and the Orange in Australia and New Zealand, 1843—Malone (R. E.) Three Years' Cruise in the Australian Colonies, 1854—How to Farm and Settle in Australia, *map and plates*, 1856 ; and 1 other (5)

616 Shortland (Edw.) Southern Districts of New Zealand, *map*, 1851 —Perils, Pastimes and Pleasures of an Emigrant in Australia, &c. 1849—Woods (Dan. B.) Sixteen Months at the Gold Diggings (1851), *all in calf gilt by Riviere* (3)

617 Shortland (Edw.) Southern Districts of New Zealand, *map*, 1851 —Pyne (Rev. A.) Reminiscences of Colonial Life, 1875— Puseley (D.) Australia, Tasmania and New Zealand, 1858— Verschuur (G.) At the Antipodes, 1891 ; and 2 others (6)

618 Shortland (Edw.) Traditions and Superstitions of the New Zealanders, *second edition*, 1856—Mitchell (Sir T. L.) Australian Geography, *map, Sydney*, 1850—Jarves (J. J.) History of the Hawaiian or Sandwich Islands, 1843—Parker (H. W.) Present State of Van Diemen's Land, *map*, 1833 ; and others (8)

619 Shürman (C. W.) Vocabulary of the Parnkalla Language, spoken by the Natives inhabiting the Western Shores of Spencer's Gulf, *half morocco* *Adelaide, G. Dehane*, 1844

620 Simmonds's Colonial Magazine and Foreign Miscellany, edited by P. L. Simmonds, vol. I-IX, *maps and illustrations, half calf* 1844-46

621 South Australian Almanack for 1842, 1850 and 1852, *Adelaide* —Low's City and District of Sydney Directory for 1847, *Sydney* (4)

622 Spry (W. J. J.) The Cruise of the "Challenger," *map and illustrations, cloth, S. Low*, 1877—Hanson (Wm.) Pastoral Possessions of New South Wales, *map, Sydney*, 1889—West (Rev. T.) Ten Years in Polynesia, *portrait and maps*, 1865 (3)

623 Stenbück (Jonas) Polynesia Detecta, Dissertatio Historica, *Lundæ*, 1707—Forster (Geo.) De Plantis Esculentis Insularum Oceani Australis, *Berol.* 1786 ; and others (5)

624 Stephens (John) South Australia. The Land of Promise, an Authentic and Impartial History of the Rise and Progress of the New British Province of South Australia, by One who is going, FIRST EDITION, *maps and plates, calf gilt by Riviere* *Smith, Elder*, 1839

625 Stephens (John) History of the Rise and Progress of the New British Province of South Australia, *second edition, maps and plates, calf gilt, by Riviere* *ib.* 1839

626 Stirling (A. W.) The Never Never Land, a Ride in South Queensland, *illustrated*, 1884—South Sea Bubbles by the Earl and the Doctor, 1872—Sutherland (Rev. R.) History of the Presbyterian Church of Victoria, 1877—The Mary Ira, Yachting Expedition from Auckland to the South Sea Islands, by J. K. M. *plates*, 1867 ; and others (8)

627 Stirling (P. J.) Australian and Californian Gold Discoveries, *Edinb.* 1853—Westgarth (W.) Australia, its Rise, &c. *ib.* 1861 —Howe (Edw.) Roughing it in Van Diemen's Land, *n. d.*— Lang (J. D.) Freedom and Independence for the Golden Lands of Australia, *maps, Sydney,* 1857 ; and others (6)

628 Stokes (Com. J. Lort) Discoveries in Australia, during the Voyage of H. M. S. Beagle, 1837-43, 3 vol. *numerous maps and plates (the maps bound in a separate volume), tree-calf gilt, m. e. by Riviere* *Boone,* 1846

629 Stokes (Com. J. Lort) Discoveries in Australia, another copy, 2 vol. *cloth* *ib.* 1846

630 Stoney (Capt. H. B.) Residence in Tasmania, *plates* 1856

631 Stuart (John Mc Dowall) Journals of Explorations in Australia, 1858-62, edited by W. Hardman, *maps and plates, cloth,* 1864 —Pritchard (W. T.) Polynesian Reminiscences, *illustrated, cloth,* 1866—Landor (E. W.) The Bushman, or Life in a New Country, *plates, cloth,* 1847 (3)

632 Stuart (Mart.) De Mensch zoo als hij Voorkomt Op den Bekenden Aardbol, afgebeeld door J. Kuyper, 6 vol. *fine coloured plates of costume, half calf* *Amst. Jo. Allart,* 1802-7

633 Stuart (Mart.) De Mensch. The Series of 28 Coloured Plates, *bound in a vol. calf gilt* (1807)

634 Sturt (Capt. Ch.) Two Expeditions into the Interior of Southern Australia, 1828-31, 2 vol. *maps and plates, some coloured, tree-calf gilt, m. e. by Riviere* *Smith, Elder,* 1833

635 Sturt (Capt. Ch.) Narrative of an Expedition into Central Australia, 1844-6, 2 vol. *plates (coloured frontispiece torn), cloth* *Boone,* 1849

636 Strzelecki (P. E. de) Physical Description of New South Wales and Van Diemen's Land, *map and plates of organic remains, &c. tree-calf gilt, m. e. by Riviere* *Longmans,* 1845

637 Sweet (Robert) Flora Australasica, Plants of New Holland and the South Sea Islands, 56 *fine coloured plates, half morocco* *roy. 8vo. Ridgway,* 1827-8

638 Sweet (Robert) Flora Australasica, another copy, *coloured plates, half bound* *imp. 8vo.* 1827-8

639 Sydney's Australian Hand-Book. How to Succeed and Settle in Australia, 1848—Harrison (R.) Colonial Sketches, or Five Years in South Australia, 1862—Fowler (Frank) Southern Lights and Shadows ; Three Years' Experience in Australia, 1859—Clarke (Marcus) Old Tales of a Young Country, *Melbourne,* 1871 (4)

640 Sydney. Handbook to Sydney and Suburbs, *plan, ib. S. T. Leigh, n. d.*—Waugh and Cox's Sydney Directory, 1855—Cox and Co.'s Post Office Sydney Directory, 1857—Sydney Magazine of Science and Art, vol. I-II in 1 vol. *half bound,* 1858 ; and 1 other (5)

E

641 Tangye (R.) Reminiscences of Travel in Australia, &c. *portrait and woodcuts*, 1883—Burke and the Australian Exploring Expedition of 1860, by A. Jackson, 1862—Butler (S.) A First Year in Canterbury Settlement, *map*, 1863 — Inglis (Hon. J.) Our New Zealand Cousins, 1887 ; and others (9)

642 Tanner's Melbourne Directory for 1859—Bailliere's South Australian Gazetteer, *map, Adelaide*, 1866—Bailliere's Queensland Gazetteer, *map, Brisbane*, 1876—Bailliere's Tasmanian Gazetteer, *map, Hobart Town*, 1877—The Tasmanian Journal of Natural Science, Agriculture, Statistics, &c. vol. I, *plates, Tasmania*, 1842 ; and others (9)

643 Taplin (Rev. G.) Folklore, Manners, Customs and Languages of the South Australian Aborigines (First Series), *Adelaide*, 1879 —Wilson (T. B.) Voyage Round the World with the Wreck of the " Governor Ready," &c. 1835—Life and Speeches of D. H. Denichy, *Melbourne*, 1884—Australian Free Religious Press, edited by Jas. Pillars, 2 vol. *Sydney*, 1871-2 ; and 1 other (6)

644 Tarleton (W. W.) Collection of the Private Acts of Practical Utility in Force in New South Wales, 1832-1885, *half calf roy. 8vo. Sydney, T. Richards*, 1886

645 Tasmania. Wood's Tasmanian Almanack, 1849-1855, 7 vol. — Walch's Tasmanian Almanack, 1863-74, 12 vol. (20)

646 Tasmania. Hobart Town Almanack for 1830, *J. Ross*—Van Diemen's Land Almanack and Annual for 1832 to 1838, *Melville and Ross*—Wood's V. D. Land Almanack for 1846, *Launceston, V. D. Land*—Van Diemen's Land Royal Kalendar, 1848, by J. Wood, *ib.* (10)

647 Tasmanian Almanack for 1828, *half bound, Hobart Town*—Hobart Town Almanack, 1830-1832 (*map in latter torn*), 1834 and 1835, *J. Ross*—Van Diemen's Land Almanack for 1833, *Hobart Town, H. Melville*—Van Diemen's Land Annual for 1835-6 ; and 1 other (8)

648 Tasmanian (The) Almanack for 1828 *Hobart Town*

649 Taylor (Rev. R.) Te Ika a Maui ; or New Zealand and its Inhabitants, *second edition, numerous illustrations, cloth W. Mackintosh*, 1870

650 Taylor (Rev. R.) New Zealand and its Inhabitants, FIRST EDITION, *map and illustrations, half calf gilt*, 1855—Torrens (R.) Colonization of South Australia, *map, half calf*, 1835 (2)

651 Taylor (W. C.) Jottings on Australia, 1872—Forbes (Anna) Insulinde, Experiences of a Naturalist's Wife in the Eastern Archipelago, 1887—Ranken (W. H. L.) The Dominion of Australia, 1874—Eden (Ch. H.) My Wife and I in Queensland, 1872 ; and others (6)

652 Technologist (The) a Monthly Record of Science applied to Art and Manufacture, edited by P. Lund Simmonds, vol. I-VI, *woodcuts (binding broken)* *Kent & Co.* 1861-66

653 Teichelmann (C. G.) and C. W. Schurmann. Outlines of a Grammar, Vocabulary and Phraseology of the Aboriginal Language of South Australia, *Adelaide*, 1840—Threlkeld (L. E.) an Australian Grammar, *Sydney*, 1834—Moore (C. J.) Descriptive Vocabulary of the Language in Common Use amongst the Aborigines of Western Australia, *half bound, W. Orr*, 1842 (3)

654 Teichelmann (C. G.) and C. W. Schürmann, Outlines of a Grammar, Vocabulary and Phraseology of the Aboriginal Language of South Australia, *half morocco*
Adelaide, published by the Authors, 1840

655 Tench (Capt. Watkin) Narrative of the Expedition to Botany Bay, with an Account of New South Wales, etc. 1789

656 Tench (Capt. W.) Narrative of the Expedition to Botany Bay, with an Account of New South Wales, etc. *Debrett*, 1789— Capt. Inglefield's Narrative concerning the Loss of H.M.S. "Centaur," *J. Murray*, 1783—Account of the Loss of H.M.S. "Deal Castle" off the Island of Porto Rico, 1780, *ib.* 1787 ; in 1 vol. *calf gilt*

657 Tenison-Woods (Rev. J. E.) Fish and Fisheries of New South Wales, 45 *plates, cloth*   *imp. 8vo. Sydney T. Richards*, 1883

658 Tenison-Woods (Rev. J. E.) Fish and Fisheries of New South Wales, 45 *plates, half morocco*   *imp. 8vo. ib.* 1883

659 Terra Australis Cognita, or Voyages to the Terra Australis or Southern Hemisphere, during the 16th, 17th and 18th Centuries, 3 vol. *maps, calf*   *Edinb. A. Donaldson*, 1766-8

660 Terry (Chas.) New Zealand, its Advantages and Prospects as a British Colony, *map and plates, tree-calf gilt, m. e. by Riviere*
Boone, 1842

661 Terry (Chas.) New Zealand as a British Colony, *map and plates, cloth*   *Boone*, 1842

662 Therry (R.) Reminiscences of Thirty Years Residence in New South Wales and Victoria, *cloth* 1863

663 Therry (R.) Reminiscences of Thirty Years Residence in New South Wales and Victoria, *half calf gilt*   *S. Low*, 1863

664 Therry (R.) Reminiscences of Thirty Years' Residence in New South Wales and Victoria, *half calf* 1863

665 Therry (R.) Reminiscences of New South Wales and Victoria
1863

666 Thomas (Julian) Cannibals and Convicts, *cloth, Cassell*, 1886— Glimpses of Life in Victoria, by a Resident, 1872—Lang (J. D.) The Coming Event; or, Freedom and Independence for Australia, 1870 ; and others (5)

667 Thomes (Wm. H.) The Belle of Australia, *illustrated, Boston*, 1883 ---Mossman (S.) Heroes of Discovery, *portraits, Edinb.* 1868 —Bourne (H. R. Fox) Story of Our Colonies, 1869—Lang (J. D.) Origin and Migrations of the Polynesian Nation, *Sydney*, 1877 ; and others (6)

668 Thomson (Arthur S.) The Story of New Zealand, *maps and plates*, 2 vol. 1859—Lancelott (F.) Australia as it is, *fronts.* 2 vol. 1852—Braim (T. H.) History of New South Wales, 2 vol. 1846 (6)

669 Thomson (A. S.) Story of New Zealand, Past and Present, Savage and Civilized, 2 vol. *plate, Murray*, 1859—Auckland, the Capital of New Zealand and the Country Adjacent, *map and views*, 1853—Green (W. Spotswood) High Alps of New Zealand, 1883—McKillop (Lieut. H. F.) Reminiscences of Twelve Months Service, 1849 (5)

670 Thomson (Dr. Wm.) On Phthisis in Australia, *Melbourne*, 1870—Stuart (T. P. Anderson) Report on the Koch Method of Treating Tuberculosis, *Sydney*, 1891—Lithotomy, its Successes and Dangers, *Melbourne*, 1876 ; and others, Medical (12)

671 Threlkeld (L. E.) An Australian Grammar; the Language Spoken by the Aborigines of New South Wales, *brown morocco gilt, Sydney*, 1834—A Key to the Structure of the Australian Language (New South Wales), *frontispiece, brown morocco gilt, ib.* 1850 (2)

672 Threlkeld (L. E.) An Australian Grammar, comprehending the Principles and Natural Rules of the Language as Spoken by the Aborigines of New South Wales, *half calf*
                                              Sydney, Stephens & Stokes, 1834

673 Threlkeld (L. E.) An Australian Grammar   *Sydney*, 1834

674 Torrens (R.) Colonization of South Australia, *second edition, map, calf gilt, m. e. by Riviere*   *Longmans*, 1836
 . Presentation Copy from the Author to George Grote.

675 Townsend (Jo. Ph.) Rambles and Observations in New South Wales, *tree-calf extra by Riviere, Chapman & Hall*, 1849—Clacy (Mrs. Chas.) Lady's Visit to the Gold Diggings of Australia in 1852-53, *frontispiece, calf gilt by Riviere, Hurst and Blackett*, 1853 (2)

676 Train (G. J.) Young America Abroad, 1857—Ryan (Bp. V. W.) Mauritius and Madagascar, 1864—The Land of Promise, or My Impressions of Australia, 1854—Ranken (W. H. L.) The Dominion of Australia, 1874 ; and others (6)

677 Transactions of the Entomological Society of New South Wales, vols. I-II, *plates, half calf*   *Sydney*, 1866-73

678 Trial of Maurice Margarot for Sedition, *portrait*, 1794—Trial of Jos. Gerrald for Sedition, *portrait, Edinb.* 1794—Trial of Thomas Fyshe Palmer, Unitarian Minister, for Sedition, *half bound, Perth*, 1793-—Fatal Effects of Gambling Exemplified in the Murder of Mr. Weare, and the Trial and Fate of John Thurtell, *plates, T. Kelly*, 1824 ; and others (6)

679 Trollope (Anthony) Australia and New Zealand, 2 vol. *maps, half bound*   *Chapman & Hall*, 1873

680 Tucker (G. A.) Lunacy in Many Lands, *cloth*
                            thick imp. 8vo. Sydney, C. Potter, 1887

681 Tuckey (J. H.) Account of a Voyage to Establish a Colony at Port Philip, New South Wales   1805

682 Ullathorne (Bp.) The Endowments of Man, *second edition (auto-graph letter inserted), Burns & Oates, 1882*—Hearn (W. E.) Government of England, *Melbourne*, 1867 ; &c. (4)

683 Ungewitter (Dr. J. H.) Australië en Zijne Bewoners, 2 vol. *plates, Haarlem, 1854*—Muller (Dr. S.) Reizen en Onder-zoekingen in den Indischen Archipel, 2 vol. in 1, *Amst. F. Muller,* 1857—Catalogus der Verzameling Vankaarten van het Ministerie van Marine, *'S Gravenhage,* 1872 ; &c. (9)

684 Vagabond Papers (The) [by Julian Thomas], 5 vol.—Old Mel-bourne Memories—Streeter on Gold ; and other Popular Books on Australia (19)

685 Vaux (Jas. Hardy) Memoirs, written by Himself, 2 vol. *half morocco,* 1819—Melville (H.) Narrative of Adventures in the South Seas, 1847 ; and others (5)

686 Victoria. Department of Agriculture, Annual Report, 1873-5, 3 vol.; Transactions of the Royal Society of Victoria, 1860, 1865-6, 2 vol. ; Victoria Prize Essays, 1860 ; Victorian Gazetteer, 1865 and 1870, 2 vol. ; Victorian Men of the Time, 1882—Statistical Register of Victoria, 1854—Illus-trated Handbook of Victoria, 1886 ; and 1 other (12)

687 Victoria. Illustrated Handbook, 1886—Statistical Register of Victoria, 1855—Victorian Government Prize Essays, 1860—Story (W.) Essay upon the Agriculture of Victoria, *map, Melbourne,* 1861 ; and others on the same Colony (20)

688 Victoria. Illustrated Handbook of Victoria, Australia, *map and plates, crimson morocco extra imp. 8vo. Melbourne, J. Ferres,* 1886

689 Victorian Review (The) Edited by H. Mortimer Franklyn, Nov. 1879 to Oct. 1880, 2 vol. *calf gilt, m. e.*
imp. 8vo. Melbourne

690 VICTORIAN YEAR BOOK (The) Containing a Digest of the Statistics of the Colony, by H. H. Hayter, from the Com-mencement in 1873 to 1892 (vol. I), 13 vol. *bound and half bound, and 10 vol. unbound Melbourne and London*

691 VICTORIAN YEAR BOOK (The), from 1873 to 1885-6, and 1888-9 ; (and Dups. 1876-7, 1880-1, 1831-2), 18 vol. *(vol. I half bound, remainder unbound) ib.*

692 Vidal (Mrs. F.) Tales for the Bush 1852

693 Vidal (Mrs.) Bengala ; or Some Time Ago, 2 vol. *cloth,* 1860—Colonial Adventures and Experiences, by a University Man, 1871—Hughes (W.) The Australian Colonies, 1852 ; &c. (10)

694 Voyage of Governor Phillip to Botany Bay, with the Journals of Lieuts. Shortland, Watts, etc., with an Account of their New Discoveries, *frontispiece, calf*
Dublin, United Company of Booksellers, n. d.

695 Wakefield (E. J.) Adventure in New Zealand, from 1839 to 1844, 2 vol. *tree-calf extra, m. e. by Riviere J. Murray,* 1845

696 Wakefield. Adventure in New Zealand. Another copy, 2 vol. *half calf* 1845

697 Walch's Tasmanian Almanac, 1865-6-7—Australian Almanacs, 1860, '4, '5, '7 and 1874—Pugh's Queensland Almanack, 1865 ; and other Colonial Almanack s, etc. (20)

698 Wallace (A. R.) The Malay Archipelago, *maps and illustrations*, 1872—Curr (E. M.) Pure Saddle-Horses and how to Breed them in Australia, *Melbourne*, 1863—Hursthouse (Ch.) Account of the Settlement of New Plymouth in New Zealand, *plates*, 1849—Loch (H. B.) Occurrences during Lord Elgin's Second Embassy to China, 1860, 1870 ; and others   (6)

699 Warburton (Col. P. E.) Journey Across the Western Interior of Australia, *map, portrait and illustrations, half calf gilt, Sampson Low*, 1875—Dutton (Fr.) South Australia and its Mines, *map and plates, cloth, Boone*, 1846—Dawson (Rob.) Present State of Australia, *half calf, Smith, Elder*, 1830   (3)

700 Ward (Rev. R.) Life Among the Maories, 1872—Just (P.) Australia, 1851-57, *map, Dundee*, 1859—Martineau (John) Letters from Australia, 1869—Lyme (J.) Nine Years in Van Diemen's Land, *Dundee*, 1848—M'Combie (Thos.) Australian Sketches. The Gold Discovery. Bush Graves, etc. 1861 ; &c.   (6)

701 Wentworth (W. C.) Description of the Colony of New South Wales and its Settlements in Van Diemen's Land, 1819—[O'Hara] History of New South Wales, *second edition*, 1818, in 1 vol. *calf gilt*

702 Wentworth (W. C.) Description of the Colony of New South Wales and its dependent Settlements in Van Diemen's Land, *cuttings inserted at end, half bound*   1819

703 Wentworth (W. C.) Description of the Colony of New South Wales, *second edition, view and map, calf*, 1820—Swainson (W.) New Zealand and its Colonization, *map, half calf*, 1859—Widowson (H.) Present State of Van Diemen's Land, *map, calf*, 1829—Melville (H.) Present State of Australia, *half morocco*, 1851   (4)

704 Wentworth (W. C.) Statistical Account of the British Settlements in Australasia, 2 vol. *third edition, maps, and view of Sydney, cloth*   *Whittaker*, 1824

705 West (John) History of Tasmania, 2 vol. *cloth*
       Tasmania, H. Dowling, 1852

706 Westgarth (Wm.) Australia Felix, an Account of the Settlement of Port Phillip, New South Wales, *map and plates, calf gilt, by Riviere*   *Edinb. Oliver and Boyd*, 1848

707 Westgarth (Wm.) Victoria and the Australian Gold Mines in 1857, *maps*, 1857—Rae (W. Fraser) Business of Travel, 1891—Rowe (Rich.) Roughing it in Van Diemen's Land, *n. d.;* and others   (8)

708 Westgarth (Wm.) The Colony of Victoria, *map*, 1864—[Stephens (John)] The Land of Promise, South Australia, *map*, 1839—Woolls (Wm.) Contribution to the Flora of Australia, *Sydney*, 1867 ; and others   (7)

709 Westgarth (Wm.) The Colony of Victoria, its History, Commerce and Gold Mining, *map, cloth*, 1864 — Tangye (R.) Reminiscences of Travel in Australia, America and Egypt, *illustrated*, 1884—Maconochie (Capt.) Thoughts on Convict Management, *Hobart Town*, 1838—Plimsoll (S.) On Cattle Ships, *illustrated*, 1890 ; and others   (6)

710 Westgarth (Wm.) Victoria; late Australia Felix, *map, cloth,*
 Edinb. Oliver and Boyd, 1853—Half a Century of Australasian
 Progress, *presentation copy, cloth, Sampson Low,* 1889 (2)
711 White (John) Voyage à la Nouvelle Galles du Sud, &c. en 1787-9
 traduit par C. Pougens, *half morocco, Paris,* 1795—Voyage du
 Gouverneur Phillip à Botany-Bay traduit de l'Anglois, *ib.*
 1791—L'Australie, Découverte, Colonisation, Civilisation, *half
 morocco, Tours,* 1880—Topinard, Les Races Indigènes de
 l'Australie, *Paris,* 1872 ; and 1 other (5)
712 Whitehead (A.) Treatise on Practical Surveying applicable to
 New Zealand and other Colonies, 1848—Erskine (J. E.)
 Cruise Among the Islands of the Western Pacific, *maps and
 plates, cloth,* 1853 (2)
713 Widowson (Henry) Present State of Van Diemen's Land, *map,*
 1829—Jeffreys (Lt. Ch.) Geographical and Descriptive Delineations of the Island of Van Diemen's Land, 1820—
 Narrative of the Sufferings of T. F. Palmer and W. Skirving
 during a Voyage to New South Wales, 1794, on board the
 "Surprise" Transport, *Camb.* 1797, *all half bound* (3)
714 Wilkinson (G. B.) South Australia, its Advantages and Resources, *maps, tree-calf extra, m. e. by Riviere J. Murray,* 1848
715 Williams (Rev. John) Missionary Enterprises in the South Sea
 Islands, *portrait, map and illustrations, half calf gilt,* 1837—
 Prout (E.) Life of the Rev. John Williams, *portrait, cloth,*
 1843 (2)
716 Williams (Thos.) Fiji and the Fijians, 2 vol. *plates,* 1858—Hort
 (Mrs. A.) Hena; or, Life in Tahiti, 2 vol. 1866—Vidal (Mrs.)
 Bengala ; or, Some Time Ago, 2 vol. 1860 ; and others (8)
717 Williams (Wm.) Vocabulary of the Language of the Adelaide
 and other Friendly Tribes of South Australia, *half morocco,
 Adelaide,* 1839—Grammatical Introduction to the Study of
 the Aboriginal Language of Western Australia (*printed without title ?) half bound, Perth, W. A.* 1841 (2)
718 Williams (Wm.) Dictionary of the New Zealand Language, and
 a Concise Grammar, *second edition Williams and Norgate,* 1852
719 Williams (Wm.) Dictionary of the New Zealand Language, and
 a Concise Grammar, and Colloquial Sentences, *first and second
 editions,* 2 vol. *cloth* *Paihia,* 1844, *Lond.* 1852
720 Wills (W. J.) Successful Exploration through the Interior of
 Australia, *map and frontispiece, half calf,* 1863—Atkinson
 (Jas.) Account of Agriculture and Grazing in New South
 Wales, *maps and plates, half bound,* 1826 (2)
721 Wine. The Vine, and How to Make Wine from Australian
 Grapes, *Geelong, Heath and Cordell,* 1859—Kelly (A. C.) Wine
 Growing in Australia, *Adelaide,* 1867—Gurgot (Dr. Jules)
 Culture of the Vine and Wine Making, *Melbourne,* 1865—
 Busby (Jas.) Culture of the Vine in New South Wales, 1840 ;
 and others (6)
722 Withers (W. B.) History of Ballarat, *folding plan, Ballarat,* 1870
 —The Friend of Australia, by a Retired Officer, *map and
 coloured plates,* 1836—Official Handbook of New Zealand,
 edited by Sir Julius Vogel, *plates,* 1875 ; and others (6)

723 Wood (G. H.) Poems, *Douglas, I. of M.* 1853—Forster (Wm.)
The Weir Wolf, 1876—The Kentish Coronal, edited by
H. G. Adams, *frontispiece*, 1841—Mackay (Ch.) The Lump
of Gold, 1856—Cambridge Prize Poems, 1828 ; &c.   (10)

724 Woods (Rev. J. E. Tenison) History of the Discovery and Ex-
ploration of Australia, 2 vol. *map and frontispiece, cloth,
Sampson Low,* 1865 — Geological Observations in South
Australia, *woodcuts,* 1862   (3)

725 Woolls (Wm.) Contribution to the Flora of Australia, *Sydney,*
1867—Moore (Ch.) Census of the Plants of New South
Wales, *ib.* 1884—Potts (T. H.) Scraps of Natural History
Gathered in New Zealand, *plates, Christchurch,* 1882—Hutton
(J. W.) Catalogues of the New Zealand Diptera, Orthoptera,
Hymenoptera, *New Zealand,* 1881 ; and others   (8)

726 Wyld's Map of Tasmania, 1859—Road Map of New South
Wales, *Sydney*—Cross's New Chart of New South Wales—
Munro's Mining Map of Sandhurst—Philips New Map of
Australia ; and other Maps   (11)

727 Yate (Rev. Wm.) Account of New Zealand, *portrait, map and
plates,* 1835—Barker (Lady) Station Life in New Zealand,
1870—Campbell (F. A.) A Year in the New Hebrides, &c.
plates, Geelong, 1874—Eden (C. H.) My Wife and I in
Queensland, 1872 ; and others   (7)

728 Yate (Rev. W.) Account of New Zealand   1835

729 York Gate Library, formed by Mr. S. Wm. Silver (Catalogue of
the) by E. A. Petherick, *second edition, vellum, uncut edges*
imp. 8vo. 1886

730 Zeichelmann (C. G.) and C. W. Schürmann, Outlines of a
Grammar, Vocabulary and Phraseology of the Aboriginal
Language of South Australia
Adelaide, published by the Authors, 1840

731 Zimmermann (Dr. W. F. A.) Die Inseln des indischen und
Stillen Meeres, 3 vol. *numerous illustrations, half bound*
Berlin, 1863-5

732 Zoological and Acclimatisation Society of Victoria (Proceedings),
vol. I to IV, *cloth*   *Melbourne,* 1872-75

733 Zoological and Acclimatisation Society, another copy, 4 vol.
(wanting vol. III)   1872-5

QUARTO.

734 New Discoveries in the Great Pacific Ocean (*extracted from
Cook's Geography*), *map and plates, half calf, with all faults, n. d.*

735 Neumayer (Geo.) Results of the Meteorological Observations
taken in the Colony of Victoria 1859-62, and of the Nautical
Observations at the Flagstaff Observatory, Melbourne 1858-
62, *cloth*   *Melbourne, John Ferres,* 1864

736 Neumayer (Geo.) Discussion of the Meteorological and Magnetical Observations at the Flagstaff Observatory, Melbourne,
1858-63, *boards*   *Mannheim,* 1867

737 New South Wales Album, 26 *coloured plates, cloth*
                              oblong. Troedel and Co. 1878
738 Nixon (Fr.) Twelve Views in Adelaide and its Vicinity, South
     Australia, *drawn, etched and printed by F. R. Nixon, half bound*
                              oblong. (Adelaide), 1845
739 Owen (Rich.) History of British Fossil Reptiles, parts 1-3, *plates,*
     Lond. for the author, 1850—Hall (Marshall) Memoirs (and New
     Memoir), 2 vol. *plates,* 1837-43 ; and others   (8)
740 Oxley (John) Journals of Two Expeditions into the Interior of
     New South Wales, 1817-18, *maps and views (some coloured),*
     calf gilt, by J. Clarke   *J. Murray,* 1820
741 Oxley (John) Expeditions into New South Wales, another
     copy, *half bound (broken)*   1820
742 PARKINSON (SYDNEY) JOURNAL OF A VOYAGE TO THE SOUTH
     SEAS in H.M.S. Endeavour, *portrait, map and plates, half*
     bound   *roy. 4to.* 1773
743 PHILLIP (GOVERNOR A.) VOYAGE TO BOTANY BAY, with an
     account of the Colonies of Port Jackson and Norfolk Island,
     portrait, maps and coloured plates, half morocco gilt, g. e.
                              J. Stockdale, 1789
744 Photograph Views, Maps of Australia, &c. Coloured Engravings,
     Portraits, &c. *in portfolio*
745 Punch in Sydney with his inexhaustible Bottle, nos. 1-4, Jan.
     3-24, 1857—Melbourne Punch's Almanack for 1859—Punch
     or the Sydney Charivari, nos. 1, 4, 6 and 7, Sept.-Nov. 1856
     —Spirit of the Age, nos. 5-8, *Sydney,* 1855—Second Annual
     Report of the Australian Botanic and Horticultural Society,
     Sydney, 1850—Illustrated Sydney Journal, nos. 3 and 5, 1855
     —The Sydney Sketch Book, *humourous illustrations, various*
     nos. 1855 ; *in 1 vol. cloth*
746 Quatrefages (A de) Les Polynesiens et leurs Migrations, *boards*
                              Paris, A. Bertrand, s. d.
747 Quiros (Pedro Ferdinandez de) Historia del descubrimiento de la
     Regiones Austriales, publicada por D. Justo Zaragoza, 2 vol.
     half morocco
     sm. 4to. Bibl. Hisp. Ultramarina Madrid, M. G. Hernandez, 1876
748 Richardson (Wm.) Catalogue of 7,385 Stars, chiefly in the
     Southern Hemisphere from Observations made in 1822-26 at
     the Observatory of Paramatta, New South Wales, *boards*
                              W. Clowes, 1835
749 Ridley (Rev. Wm.) Kamilaroi, Dippil, and Turrubul ; Languages
     Spoken by the Aborigines, *plates, calf gilt*
                              sm. 4to. Sydney, T. Richards, 1866
750 Ridley (Rev. Wm.) Kamilaroi, Dippil and Turrubul, another copy,
     morocco   *Sydney,* 1866
751 Ridley (Rev Wm.) Kamilaroi, and other Australian Languages,
     with Songs, Traditions, Laws and Customs of the Australian
     Race, *frontispiece, cloth   New South Wales, T. Richards,* 1875
752 Ridley (Rev. Wm.) Kamilaroi, another copy   1875

753 Rosenberg (C. B. H. von) Reistochten naar de Geelvinkbaai of Nieuw-Guinea in de Jaren 1869 en 1870, *maps and plates (birds coloured) brown morocco, g. e.*
'*S Gravenhage, M. Nijhoff,* 1875

754 Rümker (Carl) Mittlere Ö̈rter von 12000 Fixsternen für den Anfang von 1836, *oblong, Hamb.* 1852—The same, Preliminary Catalogue of Fixed Stars of the Southern Hemisphere observed at Paramatta, *ib.* 1832—Australien nach dem Stande der Geographischen Kenntniss in 1871, *maps, Gotha,* 1871 ; and others (4)

755 Sadleir (Rich.) The Aborigines of Australia, 8 *plates, cloth*
Sydney, T. Richards, 1883

756 SEEMANN (BERTHOLD) FLORA VITIENSIS ; a Description of the Plants of the Viti or Fiji Islands, 100 *beautifully coloured plates, cloth* *L. Reeve,* 1865-73

757 Sevarambes. Historie der Sevarambes, Volkeren die een Gedeelte van het darde Vast-Land bewoonen gemeenlyk Zuidland genaamd, *copper-plate engravings,* 4 *parts, Amst. W. de Coup,* 1701—Sadeur (Jac.) Nieuwe Reize na het Zuid-Land, *ib.* 1701 ; *in 1 vol. boards* *sm. 4to*

758 Sevarambes. Another copy, in 1 vol. *vellum* *sm. 4to*

759 Smith (J. E.) Specimen of the Botany of New Holland, vol. I *(all published),* 16 *coloured plates by Jas. Sowerby,* 1793—Shaw (G.) Zoology of New Holland, vol. I *(all published),* 12 *coloured plates by Jas. Sowerby,* 1794 ; in 1 vol. *half morocco*

760 Smyth (R. Brough) The Aborigines of Victoria, with Notes relating to the Habits of the Natives of other Parts of Australia and Tasmania, *numerous illustrations,* 2 vol. *cloth sup. imp. 8vo. Melbourne and London,* 1878

761 Smyth (R. Brough) The Gold Fields and Mineral Districts of Victoria, *plates, cloth sup. imp. 8vo. Melbourne, J. Ferres,* 1869

762 Sonnerat. Voyage à la Nouvelle Guinée, 120 *plates, old calf*
Paris, Ruault, 1776

763 Sonnerat. Reise nach Neuguinea, aus dem Französische übersetzt von J. P. Ebeling, *copper-plate engravings, boards Leipzig,* 1777

764 Sydney. Landscape Scenery illustrating Sydney and Port Jackson, &c. N. S. W. *title and* 17 *views, morocco gilt*
oblong. Sydney, J. Sands, n. d.

765 Sydney Punch, vol. I, *numerous illustrations, half bound, very scarce*
Sydney, E. Ray, 1864

766 Sydney Fun (The) a Humourous, Quizzical and Satirical Journal, nos. 1-57 *(wanting nos.* 6 *and* 20), in 1 vol. *cloth*
Sydney, 1880-81

767 Tench (Capt. Watkin) Complete Account of the Settlement at Port Jackson, New South Wales, *map, half calf*
G. Nicol, 1793

768 Terres Australes (Histoire des Navigations aux), Contenant ce que l'on Sçait des Mœurs et des Productions des Contrées découvertes jusqu'à ce Jour, 2 vol. *old calf*
Paris, Durand, 1756

769 Turnbull (John) Voyage Round the World, 1800-1804 (Botany Bay, Norfolk Island, etc.) *half calf*   *A. Maxwell*, 1813

770 Vancouver (Capt. Geo.) Voyage of Discovery to the North Pacific Ocean and Round the World, 1790-5, 3 vol. *plates, russia gilt (binding broken)*   *Robinson*, 1798

771 Victorian Statutes (The) Published by Authority, 4 vol. *cloth*   *Melbourne, J. Ferres*, 1866

772 Views, Plain and Coloured, of Sydney, N. S. W. (6)—Large Panoramic Photographic Views of Sydney, etc.   *a parcel*

773 Voice (The) of the Wilderness   *Sydney, W. Nation*, 1846-48

774 Voyage de Découvertes aux Terres Australes sur les Corvettes le Géographe, Le Naturaliste et la Goelette le Casuarina, 1800-1804, rédigé par F. Péron, 2 vol. *4to and folio atlas of maps and plates (some coloured), boards, uncut*   *Paris, Impr. Imp.* 1807

775 Voyage de Découvertes. Another copy, 2 vol. *calf 4to, and folio atlas, half calf*   1807

776 Voyages and Discoveries (General Collection of) made by the Portuguese and Spaniards in the 15th and 16th Centuries, *maps and plates, half morocco*   *W. Richarson, etc.* 1789

777 Voyages and Travels (New and General Collection of) in Europe, Asia, Africa and America, 4 vol. *numerous maps and plates, T. Astley*, 1745—Wilson (Jas.) Missionary Voyage to the Southern Pacific, 1799 ; and others   (10)

778 Voyages autour du Monde et en Oceanie par Bougainville, Cook, La Pérouse, Marion, etc. *numerous illustrations, half morocco, Paris, J. Bry*, 1853—La Tour du Monde (Java, Australia, New Guinea, The Pacific), *illustrated (no title), half morocco* (2)

779 Walch (Garnet) Victoria in 1880, *illustrated by Chas. Turner, cloth gilt*   *Melbourne, G. Robertson*

780 Wales (Wm.) and Wm. Bayly. The Original Astronomical Observations made in the Course of a Voyage towards the South Pole, and Round the World, in the "Endeavour" and "Resolution," 1772-75, *map and plates, Strahan*, 1777 ; Astronomical Observations made in the Voyages of Byron, Wallis, Carteret and Cook, in 1 vol. *with maps of New Zealand and Eastern Coast of New Holland, drawn by Captain Cook. C. Buckton*, 1788, *in 1 vol. half calf*

781 Western Australia. Ongeluckige Voyagie van het Schip Batavia, uytgevaren onder 't beleydt van den E. François Pelsaert na Oost-Indien, etc. en 1628-29, ORIGINAL EDITION, lit. goth. *copper-plate engravings by Corn. Van Sichem, half morocco, very scarce*   *sm. 4to. Amst. G. J. Saeghman, K. O.* (1630)

782 Western Australia. Ongeluckige Voyagie van 't Schip Batavia ; nevens een Treurblyende Ongheluck des Oost-Indische Compagnies Dienaers in 't Jaer 1636 in 't Conincklijcke Hof van Siam onder E. Jeremias Van Vliet, etc. lit. goth. *copper-plate engravings (stained), half morocco sm. 4to. Amst. J. Jansz*, 1647

783 Westmacott (Capt. R. M.) Sketches in Australia, drawn on stone by W. Spreat, 18 *plates, half bound* Exeter, 1848

784 WHITE (JOHN) JOURNAL OF A VOYAGE TO NEW SOUTH WALES, *with* 65 *plates of Natural Productions,* COLOURED, *J. Debrett,* 1790—Extracts of Letters from Governor Phillip to Lord Sydney, with a Description of Norfolk Islands, etc. *ib.* 1791—Copies and Extracts of Letters from Governor Phillip, giving an Account of New South Wales, 1792, *in* 1 *vol. old French red morocco gilt, g. e. (Derome),* FINE COPY

785 White. Journal. Another copy, the PLATES COLOURED, *russia gilt, g. e. Fonthill copy* Debrett, 1790

786 White. Journal. Another copy, *plain plates, calf* ib. 1790

787 Wilson (Capt. Jas.) Missionary Voyage to the Southern Pacific Ocean, 1796-98, *maps, charts and views, half calf*
T. Chapman, 1799

788 Wilson. Missionary Voyage. Another copy, *calf* 1799

789 Wilson (Hon. J. Bowie) Report on Lord Howe Island, *maps and plates, cloth, Sydney,* 1882—Archer (W. H.) Patents and Patentees (Victoria), 1854-66, *Melbourne,* 1868—Catalogue of the Parliamentary Library of Queensland, *Brisbane,* 1883—Catalogue of the Natural and Industrial Products of New South Wales, *Sydney,* 1854 ; and others (7)

790 Zoology of the Beagle. Fossil Mammalia, Mammalia, Birds, Fishes and Reptiles, 3 vol. *numerous plates, coloured and plain, half morocco* 1839-43

MANUSCRIPTS.

791 New South Wales. JOURNAL of TRANSACTIONS on NORFOLK ISLAND and in NEW SOUTH WALES Generally, with copies of all Correspondence, List of Settlers, &c. 1791-1794, by PHILIP GIDLEY KING, LIEUT.-GOVERNOR, UNPUBLISHED MSS. copied from Documents in the Record Office, etc. divided into 4 vol. *half morocco ;* and 2 vol. *unbound* 4to

*** Historical MSS. of great interest and importance for the History of the Colony.

792 BANKS (SIR JOSEPH) AUTOGRAPH MANUSCRIPT JOURNAL of his VOYAGE in the ENDEAVOUR with CAPT. COOK, UNPUBLISHED, 2 vol. *calf* 4to. 1770

793 MUTINY OF THE BOUNTY. LETTERS of CAPT. W. BLIGH, COMMANDER of the BOUNTY, to Sir Joseph Banks, 1787-8 (20) ; Papers relating to the Loss of the Vessel, Plan for the Voyage, Captain Piper's Narrative of the late Mutineers settled on Pitcairn Island, &c. *a parcel*

*** An interesting and valuable collection.

794 PHILLIP (ARTHUR) GOVERNOR OF BOTANY BAY. SERIES of 14 AUTOGRAPH LETTERS addressed to SIR JOSEPH BANKS, giving full Accounts of the Colony, and especially of its Natural Products ; also *extracts from a journal, &c.* AN INTERESTING AND VALUABLE COLLECTION *written between* 1787 *and* 1790, *mostly dated from Sydney* *a parcel*

Manuscripts—*continued.*

795 Western Australia. A Description of the Colony, its Inhabitants, Products, Commercial Advantages, in a Series of Letters (Copies) by Mrs. Eliza Shaw to her friends in England, June, 1833, *sepia drawing of Mrs. Shaw's cottage*—Verzeichniss von Circumpolar Sternen für Repsoldo Sternwarte, 1811—Newspaper Cuttings relating to Australia, in a vol. (3)

796 Leupe (P. A.) De Reizen der Nederlanders naar het Zuidland of Nieuw-Holland in de 17ᵉ en 18ᵉ leuw, *numerous MS. notes and additions by the Author, Amst.* 1868—Journal van Tasman's Reis, 1642, door Jac. Swart, *numerous MS. notes and additions, ib.* 1860 (2)

797 Bulam. Form of a Constitution of Government for a Colony about to be established on the Island of Bulam, in Africa—Report of the Bulam Association, 1792—Autograph Letter of P. Le Mesurier, one of the Trustees of the Bulam Colony, 27 Dec. 1792 (3)

FOLIO.

798 Lycett. Views in Australia, 2 *maps and* 50 *fine coloured views, half green morocco* *oblong.* 1825

799 Mammals of Australia, illustrated by Mrs. Harriett Scott and Mrs. Helena Forde, with Account of all the species hitherto described by G. Krefft, 15 *plates* *roy. fol.* Sydney, T. Richards, 1871

800 Mammals of Australia. Another copy 1871

801 Meredith (L. Anne) My Bush Friends in Tasmania, *coloured plates (some stained, one loose), cloth* Day & Son, 1860

802 Newspapers published in New South Wales in 1875, 88 *specimen Nos. with a printed list of all their names, half bound atlas fol.*

803 New Zealand Journal (The) for 1840, 1842, 1843, 1844, 1847, and 1848, in 4 vol. *half bound, very scarce* Lond. 1840-8

804 Picturesque Atlas of Australasia, edited by the Hon. Andrew Garran, *maps and many hundred illustrations,* 3 vol. *morocco gilt* *roy. fol.* 1886

805 Picturesque Atlas of Australasia, parts 23-32, 38 and 42

806 Premier Livre de l' Histoire de la Navigation aux Indes Orientales, par les Hollandois et des choses à eux advenues, etc. par G. M. A. W. L. *première edition, map on title, and copperplate engravings in the text, paper covers, uncut edges* Amst. C. Nicolas, 1598

807 Prout (J. S.) Tasmania Illustrated, vol. I, 12 *lithograph views, and* 2 *loose* *imp. folio.* Hobart Town, 1844

808 Rotomahana, and the Boiling Springs of New Zealand, 16 Photographic Views by D. L. Mundy, with Descriptive Notes by J. von Hochstetter, *cloth* *S. Low*, 1875

809 Scott (A. W.) Australian Lepidoptera and their Transformations, drawn from the Life by Harriett and Helena Scott, 9 *plates, containing numerous coloured details, half morocco*
atlas 4to. Van Voorst, 1864

810 Shipley (Conway) Sketches in the Pacific, the South Sea Islands, 25 *tinted plates (some foxed), boards* 1851

811 Sidney's Emigrant's Journal, 1849—Shipping Gazette (The) and Sydney General Trade List, vol. VI and VIII, *Sydney*, 1850-2 —Dicker's Mining Record, vol. II, III, X, XI, XII, in 3 vol. *Melbourne*, 1883-9 (6)

812 Sidney (Sir Philip) Arcadia Moderniz'd, by Mrs. Stanley, LARGE PAPER, *old calf* 1725

813 South Australian Record (The), Nos. 1-29 in 1 vol. *half bound, Lond.* 1837-39—South Australian Colonist, Nos. 1-29 in 1 vol. *half bound, ib.* 1840—Australian and New Zealand Gazette, Jan.-Dec. 1853, in 2 vol. *half bound* (4)

814 Southern Cross (The), a Weekly Journal of Politics, Literature, and Social Progress, Nos. 1-46, Oct. 1, 1859, August 11, 1860, in 1 vol. (*all published), half bound* *Sydney*

815 Stockwhip (The), vol. I-III, *half bound, Sydney*, 1875-6—The Spectator, vol. I-IV, in 3 vol. *Melbourne*, 1865-7 ; and 1 other (7)

816 Trial of Sir Roger Tichborne, Bart. by Dr. Kenealy, *numerous illustrations*, vol. II, 1876—National Australian Convention, Official Record of the Convention and Debates, 1891—Imperial Federation, Journal of the Imperial Federation League, vol. I, 1886—The Victorian Independent, Nos. 1-11, in 1 vol. *half bound, Melbourne*, 1870-1 (4)

817 Tulloch (D.) The Gold Diggings of Victoria, *engraved and published by Thos. Ham, 5 views and illustrated wrapper*
oblong. Melbourne, 1852

818 VICTORIAN PARLIAMENT. Bribery, Expulsion of Members of Parliament, Contempt by Members, First Progress Report of Commission on the Destitute Act, 1883—Papers on Deadlocks in the Victorian Parliament, 1878 (3)

819 Voyage de la Corvette d'Astrolabe pendant les Années 1826-29, sous le Commandement de J. Dumont D'Urville (*wants vol. II of Voyage, vol. IV of the Zoologie, all the maps, and atlas of charts*), 11 vol. 8vo of Text, and 2 folio Atlases to " Zoologie " and " Histoire," *sold with all faults*
Paris, 1830, &c.

820 Wallis (Capt.) Historical Account of the Colony of New South Wales, *map and 12 views, engraved by W. Preston, a convict, boards* *roy. folio. Ackermann*, 1821

821 WEBBER (JAS.) VIEWS IN THE SOUTH SEAS, 16 *fine coloured plates, half bound*   *atlas folio.*   *Boydell,* 1808

822 Whitehall Review (The), Nov. 1876, to Nov. 1877, 54 *portraits of female aristocracy in crayons,* 2 vol. *cloth*

823 Whitehall Review Album, Second Series, 26 *portraits in crayons, cloth*   *atlas folio.*   1877

824 Zee-Atlas (De) Oste Water-Wereld waer in vertoont Werden alle de Zee-Kusten, *numerous coloured charts, vellum gilt*   *imp. folio.*   *Amst. P. Goos,* 1676

END OF SALE.

DRYDEN PRESS : J. Davy & Sons, 137, Long Acre, London.

www.ingramcontent.com/pod-product-compliance
Lightning Source LLC
Chambersburg PA
CBHW021518090426
42739CB00007B/670